"The Global Teacher Prize is a one million dollar prize that is awarded to one exceptional teacher who has made an outstanding contribution to the profession. It was set up to shine a spotlight on the profession in order to celebrate the important role teacher's play in society. By unearthing thousands of stories of heroes that have transformed young people's lives, the prize brings to life the exceptional work of millions of teachers all over the world. In this book, some of our leading finalists give us their unique insights into how we can teach the next generation to flourish in a world that will be revolutionized by artificial intelligence, automation and new communication technologies."

"If we are to recognize the contribution of the world's teachers, we must seize every possible opportunity to give them a voice. Teachers point and guide the way, opening young people's hearts and minds, whilst preparing them for the opportunities and threats that the future will bring. Through spreading teachers' very different stories about how they light the spark of curiosity, we can help give the gift of a good education to every child."

Sunny Varkey, Founder of the Varkey Foundation and
The Global Teacher Prize, UAE

"The big picture of change – why education matters, what its purpose should be, how this can be done in a rapidly changing world - is usually owned & controlled by academics and policy-makers. Teachers are left with lots of little pictures of things to do and implement in their own classes. From some of the world's best and most recognized classroom teachers, this book shows how and why teachers must also understand and own the big pictures of change about social justice, peace, democracy, innovation and sustainability – and make these things come true in every class with every child. This is a truly uplifting book by great teachers who are also public intellectuals."

Andy Hargreaves, Thomas More Brennan Chair,
Lynch School of Education at Boston College, USA

"As our world becomes increasingly complex and divided, our need to foster communities that are healthier, more empathetic, and embrace our shared humanity has never been greater. The authors, among the most highly recognized educators in the world, give us a path forward to achieve this goal. Combining research with compelling narratives, this book demonstrates how education that is rooted in humanity can help foster a new generation of leaders – leaders who adopt a sense of responsibility to other human beings and

solve society's biggest challenges. This is a must read for educators and for anyone who has an interest in creating a better and kinder future."

Daniel Lubetzky, CEO and Founder at KIND and Empatico, Mexico

"This is an unusual education book. It is built around six individual teacher voices from schools around the world asking the same question: Can teachers make a difference to prepare us for the Fourth Industrial Revolution? Read this book to find out how passionate practitioners can have optimistic professional dialogue about what we need to do and how to transform education systems to be good for all our kids."

Pasi Sahlberg, author of Finnish Lessons 2.0, Finland

"Those who write about education tend either to celebrate or to castigate the disruptive aspects of technology. In this collection of essays, thoughtful educators reflect on how best to combine the powerful potential of the new technologies with the valuable, indeed irreplaceable qualities of excellent human teachers."

Howard Gardner, John H. and Elisabeth A. Hobbs Professor of Cognition and Education at the Harvard Graduate School of Education at Harvard University, USA

"Education is more than the communication of information, it is the impartation of wisdom, birthed by experience, to the next generation. Teaching in the Fourth Industrial Revolution opens a window beyond academics, into real life."

Dr. A. R. Bernard, Founder and Senior Pastor, Christian Cultural Center, USA

"More than just ideas, this collection of essays provides practical strategies and powerful models disrupting mediocrity within a stagnated education system. Each author offers a candid view of the challenges teachers' face due to the inequities in their classrooms, while sharing stories of hope and promise for the future. If we seek to revolutionize education and prepare children for the Fourth Industrial Revolution, this book offers great insight from the educators doing the work."

Juliet Blake, Head of Television & Curator of Special Projects, TED, USA

"This is a moment in time. How do we prepare students for the Fourth Industrial Revolution? Written by some of the world's most outstanding educators, Teaching in the Fourth Industrial Revolution: Standing at the Precipice is an insightful work on how to help students thrive. An invaluable resource for the world's educators."

C. M. Rubin, Founder, The Global Search for Education, USA

"This book makes a compelling contribution to our thinking on education in the decades ahead. The authors – all world-leading teachers – discuss how education can promote a prosperous, just and peaceful future for the world during a time of huge technological upheaval. Through topics such as social media, collaboration across sectors, and the personalization of teaching, the authors also elaborate on their individual pedagogical approaches, drawing on decades' worth of experimentation in the classroom. The result is an authoritative guide to educational practice over the next three decades."

Vikas Pota, Chief Executive, Varkey Foundation, UK

"Are you tired of seeing your students' potential go unrealized and do you feel in your heart of hearts that you could be doing so much more to preserve and protect our imperiled world in a time of unprecedented societal transformations? If so, "Teaching in the Fourth Industrial Revolution" is the book for you! With vivid, hands-on examples, the authors describe how we can work with our students, colleagues, and community partners to uplift education in the years ahead. Best of all, the authors are not afraid to advance big ideas with solid practical foundations beneath them. Here is a book that truly is essential reading for all educators who are serious about paving the way to a better future for all of our students."

Dennis Shirley, Professor of Education at the Lynch School of Education at Boston College and Editor-in-Chief of the Journal of Educational Change, USA

"Our planet is struggling to support the methods adopted and the pace of development that we aspire. Many thresholds are close to being breached because of myopic policies and wise decisions are needed to delay and defer the crises. The society needs leaders who can understand the complexities of the processes that are contributing to the problems and those that can counter these. The most critical investment our generation can make, in terms of ideas, time and resources, is in the field of education. This publication has thought provoking essays that stimulate discussion and debate on the problems and potential of education world-wide. There is understandable stress on the need for developing capacity for critical thinking in the course curriculum, delivery methods and assessment of progress from early years. The authors, each a highly recognized teacher and very passionate about nurturing global health, aim at developing empathy at the heart of the education system. This needs to be read by all educationists and policy makers."

> **Er Anuj Sinha,** Former Adviser, Department of
> Science and Technology, Government of India,
> New Delhi and Chairman, Network of
> Organisations for Science and Technology
> Communication, India

"The bedrock of a democratic country is universal; equitable public education. You cannot achieve sustainable economic and social well-being for any country unless all citizens have equal access to affordable education, ideally from two years of age onward. This book explains and demonstrates how to get that educational foundation."

> **Honourable Margaret Norrie McCain,** Canada

"Education and teaching do not conform to a single definition or one set of rules. The world is changing and education must change with it. Perhaps there can be no discussion as important to our children and the world itself, than that of how to prepare future generations to deal with global challenges. The authors share some difficulties teachers face today, but also possible solutions – including bringing the human aspect back to education in a technological and connected world."

> **Céline Cousteau,** Filmmaker and Explorer,
> Founder of CauseCentric Productions, USA

"New forces are at work in the world: accelerating globalization, technological revolutions, increasing inequalities and global warming. All call for new models of living together as responsible global citizens. This starts with education that makes a difference in the life of every child and youth, whatever their circumstances may be, and empowers them with the confidence, knowledge, ethics and empathy to contribute to their communities and societies. This is the promise of Sustainable Development Goal 4 that aims to 'ensure inclusive and equitable quality education and promote lifelong learning opportunities for all.' This book brings together six wonderful teachers who share one same passion: to make education a truly transformative experience that harnesses technology to connect, but most importantly, empowers teachers and learners through a relationship founded on respect, collaboration and creativity and the conviction that to every learning difficulty, there is a solution. This is a must read for educators, practitioners, decision-makers, parents and anyone concerned with the future of education today."

Irina Bokova, Director-General of
UNESCO (2009–2017)

"In *Teaching in the Fourth Industrial Revolution* six reflective and highly accomplished teachers ponder about the present and the future of the world and of humanity and ask: how could education best serve children so they build a better future? Drawing on years of practice, conversations with colleagues, study of classical texts in education, as well as current education research, they develop insightful and provocative answers to key questions about the present and the future of education. As they pause to ask important questions about what purpose their own teaching practice, and the practice of other teachers around the world, should serve to build a better future, these teachers embody the highest standards of any profession. Their insights have consequential implications for how to structure and support teacher practice and teacher education and lifelong learning. The valuable result of the collaboration of these teachers from four different countries exemplifies also the power of diverse groups to generate creative insights to some of the most thorny challenges of our times. Anyone interested in the future of education should read this book."

Fernando M. Reimers, Ford Foundation Professor
of the Practice of International Education and
Director Global Education Innovation Initiative
and International Education Policy Program at
the Harvard Graduate School of Education, USA

"The collective voices from effective educators around the world can be finally heard in Teaching in the Fourth Industrial Revolution. The authors, outstanding teachers themselves, reflect on their role as technology enters the classroom. They discuss the challenges of inequity, the perils of education systems that disregard teachers and their insights, and the need for society to step up and claim its place in raising our children. As they stress, human interactions remain at the core of the learning experience; the reader is invited to witness first-person accounts into exceptional teaching practices. This book is the opening line to the discussions we all need to have about education for 2030 and beyond."

Emiliana Vegas, Division Chief of Education
Inter-American Development Bank, USA

"At a time when the world is facing serious issues, this book makes clear that the solutions begin with education. By blending the perspectives of educators with diverse backgrounds, the authors show how we can improve education systems around the world to create a new era for our planet in which every child is encouraged to believe that anything is possible. Simply put, this book shines a light on how we can prepare our children and our students for the world of 2030 and beyond."

Hanan al Hroub, Recipient of the 2016
Global Teacher Prize, Palestine

"There is an old military adage that states: Time spent on reconnaissance is never wasted. Anticipating what lies around the turn in the road has always been a critical matter in any environment. The same is true in Education – only more so. Looking to the future, anticipating issues and suggesting approaches that will bring the next generation to the level of dealing with the critical and complex societal and political issues to be faced, is the challenge. Education is not only the vanguard – it is the solution. This book, by a group of very accomplished teachers and forward thinkers in education, opens the door and lets us have a look at that process. This book is a compelling and authoritative view into that process and that future."

James E. Lockyer, c.r./Q.C., Professor Faculty
of Law, Université de Moncton, Canada

"Education is the foundation for everything else that we want to achieve and the commitment of the teaching profession is to ensure free public quality education for all children. We need a democratic, professional, self-confident, well-supported and versatile teaching profession that has professional autonomy and professional capital. As these authors – and colleagues – show, it is only by building trust that we will take teaching and education forward. In these uncertain times this book comes at the right time and shows us what can be achieved if we start trusting all our teachers."

Fred van Leeuwen, Secretary General,
Education International

"The contributors to this book paint a compelling portrait of how we should approach education if we are to provide a sustainable future in a rapidly changing world. The vital lesson to learn from these teachers is the degree to which education must lead the way as governments seek to ensure that society benefits from the Fourth Industrial Revolution."

The Right Honourable Paul Martin, P.C.,
Former Prime Minister of Canada

Teaching in the Fourth Industrial Revolution

In this visionary book, written by six internationally recognized Global Teacher Prize finalists, the authors create a positive and hope-filled template for the future of education. They address the hard moral, ethical and pedagogical questions facing education today so that progress can serve society, rather than destroying it from within our classrooms.

This blueprint for education finally brings forward what has always been missing in education reform: a strong collective narrative with authentic examples from teachers on the front line. It is a holistic, personalized approach to education that harnesses the disruptions of the Fourth Industrial Revolution to better shape the future for the next generation, and ensure that every child can benefit from the ongoing transformations.

A great read for anyone who has an interest in educating our youth for these uncertain times, highlighting why teachers will always matter.

Armand Doucet, Jelmer Evers, Elisa Guerra, Dr. Nadia Lopez, Michael Soskil and **Koen Timmers** are amongst some of the world's most influential and innovative classroom teachers. As visionary and award-winning educators, they are recognized throughout the globe for their unique and groundbreaking approaches to education. Their ideas are celebrated in a number of different sectors.

Teaching in the Fourth Industrial Revolution

Standing at the Precipice

Armand Doucet, Jelmer Evers,
Elisa Guerra, Dr. Nadia Lopez,
Michael Soskil and
Koen Timmers

Routledge
Taylor & Francis Group

LONDON AND NEW YORK

First published 2018
by Routledge
2 Park Square, Milton Park, Abingdon, Oxon OX14 4RN

and by Routledge
711 Third Avenue, New York, NY 10017

Routledge is an imprint of the Taylor & Francis Group, an informa business

British Library Cataloguing-in-Publication Data
A catalogue record for this book is available from the British Library

Library of Congress Cataloging-in-Publication Data
A catalog record for this book has been requested

ISBN: 978-1-138-48324-8 (hbk)
ISBN: 978-1-138-48323-1 (pbk)
ISBN: 978-1-351-03586-6 (ebk)

Typeset in Bembo
by Apex CoVantage, LLC

Visit the companion website:
www.routledge.com/cw/doucet

Contents

Foreword

As the Fourth Industrial Revolution unfolds, it is certain that how we learn, earn, work and live will go through fundamental shifts. Many of today's education systems are already disconnected from the competences needed to function in today's labour markets and the exponential rate of technological and economic change threatens to further widen the gap between education and the demands of the global workforce. In turn, this creates barriers to individuals' ability to create value in the global economic system and, more importantly, fully realize their potential. Now more than ever, it is critical that we create a new integrated, agile, sustainable and lifelong education system that matches the needs of the future. Fortunately, entirely new ways of teaching and learning have also begun to emerge and can point the way to the future.

What does Education 4.0 look like? The forward-thinking educators in this book have developed a timely collection of insights about the future of education within the context of the Fourth Industrial Revolution. Each author has been nominated for the Global Teacher Prize for their pioneering work in education. The annual Prize is awarded by the Varkey Foundation, an innovator in leading change in education globally, including through their engagement with the World Economic Forum.

It is clear that we must reform our curricula to teach a newer range of material to youth and adults alike as technology disrupts nearly every field. In addition the ability to engage with and use technology will be critical for students. However, students must be adept not only at understanding technological change and using technology, but also in developing profoundly human skills such as leadership, social-emotional intelligence and critical thinking. If competition has defined the education of the past, collaboration, empathy and teamwork will define the education of the future. Moreover, we need to impart students with a new flexible and adaptable mind-set about learning, one that emphasizes the need for continued, lifelong learning. To embrace such a mind-set, students must learn to be curious about their changing environment and develop the resilience necessary to not just manage but to thrive on change.

The future of education content is thus neither wholly digital nor wholly human but a hybrid of both. This applies to teaching too. Embracing technology as an instrument of empowerment in the classroom can enhance teaching. Innovations in technology today make it possible to synthesize and analyse data to tailor pedagogy to individual student needs and provide feedback in real time; significantly reduce costs; allow students from drastically different parts of the world to collaborate on projects; and create platforms for sharing best practices across the world. Teachers must thus work in tandem with technology to provide holistic education that prepares students for the future. Only a strategic integration of personal coaching and digital learning can provide both the technological and human-centred skills necessary to thrive in the Fourth Industrial Revolution.

The authors in this book have shared personal experiences of the impact of technology on the nature of their work, and best practices for successfully integrating these changes in the classroom to benefit student learning. Each has discovered unique and innovative methods for using technology to amplify their teaching.

The Fourth Industrial Revolution may be driving disruption, but it is wholly in our power to address the challenges and embrace the new opportunities. In the case of education, we can harness the disruptions to yield incredibly positive results. While there is no silver bullet, creating a successful strategy to integrate technology and education to face the challenges ahead will ultimately require effective collaborations among policy-makers, educators, businesses and civil society. The remarkable educators in this book have set the stage for designing an education system that matches the needs of the future and it is my hope that all stakeholders can work together towards unlocking a new golden age in education.

Professor Klaus Schwab,
Founder and Executive Chairman,
World Economic Forum
4 December 2017

Author Biographies

Armand Doucet

 Armand Doucet is a visionary, award-winning educator, social entrepreneur and business professional. A sought-after leader, inspirational speaker, author, columnist and blogger in multiple fields, Armand has contributed to CBC, Education Partners, BrainStem Symposium, STEM Educators Symposium, Atlantic Education Summit, Teach SDGs and TedX. He has led and collaborated with teams from around the world and across different industries to success in health, education, non-profit organizations and business. Armand was the president and founder of the Ironwill Foundation and was also part of a team of teachers who brought Harry Potter to life at Riverview Middle School, connecting the school to over 1.8 million people around the globe. Recently, Armand founded *Life Lesson Learning*, which is working to change teaching worldwide by giving competencies and character development its proper place in the classroom through his Passion Projects initiative. Armand received the Canadian Prime Minister's Award for Teaching Excellence 2015, is a Meritorious Service Medal Recipient Governor General of Canada, is an Apple Distinguished Educator and Teach SDGs ambassador, and he has just recently been nominated in the Top 50 for the Global Teacher Prize. A two-time Ironman athlete, he currently is inspired by the best colleagues in the world, while teaching at Riverview High School in the Anglophone East School District of the New Brunswick Department of Education.

Jelmer Evers

Jelmer is a history teacher, writer and innovator. He teaches at an innovative school: UniC in Utrecht, the Netherlands. He proposes a renaissance of education with teachers in the lead on all levels. In 2015, his book *Flip the System* was published around the world. Evers has been nominated teacher of the year 2012 and has received several other national awards. He was nominated twice for the Global Teacher Prize in 2015 and 2016. In 2013, he edited an influential book called *Het Alternatief* (*The Alternative*) featuring articles from renowned scholars like Andy Hargreaves, Howard Gardner and Pasi Sahlberg. The book made an enormous impact and was debated in Dutch parliament a month after publication. Several policy recommendations of his have been put into practice: less standardized testing, more hybrid teachers and a strengthened professional body which runs a teacher-led €5-million innovation fund (Lerarenontwikkelfonds). Amongst others, he was also on the design team of a new teacher education institute: De Nederlandse School. In 2015, a new international book called *Flip the System: Changing education from the ground up* was published worldwide, and Swedish, English and Australian spin-offs have been published or are in the works. He is a co-founder of TEN Global: a new Global Teacher and Educator Network with Education International.

Elisa Guerra

Elisa Guerra was named the Best Educator in Latin America by the Inter-American Development Bank IDB in 2015, and was a Top 50 finalist for the Global Teacher Prize in 2015 and 2016. When she could not find a school in her hometown of Aguascalientes, Mexico, that was challenging and stimulating enough for her own children, she founded Colegio Valle de Filadelfia. Her model has been escalated, and there are now nine campuses in three countries. All over Latin America, Elisa has worked with both privileged and underprivileged children and has lectured in English and Spanish around the world. She trains teachers online and has taught more than 2,000 educators from 56 countries. She runs the Latin American chapter of The Institutes for the Achievement of Human Potential, an international NGO teaching parents how to help their children affected by a brain injury. Elisa has authored 25 textbooks for students and teachers. Pearson Education published the series for preschoolers in 2014. Her books for elementary school students followed in 2017. At her school in Aguascalientes, Elisa teaches early reading, global citizenship, social studies and technology. She is passionate about early education and special needs children. Al Jazeera featured Elisa in a 2017 documentary titled *Mexico: The Power or Early Education* for the series Rebel Education, which aim was to showcase the most innovative education initiatives from around the world.

Dr. Nadia Lopez

Founding Principal of Mott Hall Bridges Academy, Dr. Nadia Lopez is pioneering a leadership path showing underprivileged communities creating positive institutions that have global impact. Due to her work in education, Nadia has appeared on the *Ellen Show*, visited President Obama, and received the Medal of Distinction from Barnard College. In 2015, a HONY fundraiser raised $1.4 million to provide Nadia's students college trips and scholarships. Dr. Lopez is also a Black Girls Rock Change Agent, TED Speaker and the author of *The Bridge to Brilliance*, an inspirational account of the creation of a groundbreaking inner-city middle school in Brooklyn, New York. Understanding the power of programming, Nadia continues to impact the lives of children through her "She Is Me" and "I Matter" initiatives, which have served thousands of youth throughout Central Brooklyn by providing workshops, forums and mentoring. Nadia continues to influence and inspire the world through her company The Lopez Effect, which offers a blueprint for personal and organizational success.

Michael Soskil

Michael Soskil, the 2017–2018 Pennsylvania Teacher of the Year, is determined to make learning meaningful for every child and to empower students and teachers as positive change agents in their communities. As an elementary science teacher at the Wallenpaupack South Elementary School, he inspires young scientists to use their curiosity and learning to make the world a better place. His students have gained international attention for initiatives that have included designing a bridge for a rural village in Africa, connecting with students in Kansas and Greece to provide clean drinking water for hundreds of families in the Kibera slum of Nairobi, and starting a Distance Teaching Project that expanded to include videos from students on six continents sharing their learning with others. In 2012, Michael's innovative work was recognized by the White House and US National Science Foundation with the Presidential Award for Excellence in Math and Science Teaching. In 2016, he was named a Global Teacher Prize finalist and one of the top ten teachers in the world by the Varkey Foundation. His message of student empowerment and teaching through empathy has been shared with teachers, policy makers, businesspeople and students around the globe. Outside the classroom, he serves as an advisor to several NGOs and non-profit organizations focused on global education, and sits on the governing board for the Pennsylvania Teachers Advisory Committee, which is providing a pipeline to connect teacher voice education decision makers.

Koen Timmers

Koen Timmers is researcher and lecturer at PXL University College in Hasselt, Belgium. He was a Top 50 finalist in the Global Teacher Prize 2017 and 2018. In 2000, he launched his own online school Zelfstudie.com; it currently has 20,000 students. He founded the Kakuma project in which he managed to connect 100 global educators who now offer free education to African refugees via Skype. Koen is a Microsoft Expert Educator Fellow and has been speaking about technology-enhanced learning across four continents. He is one of the TeachSDGs taskforce members. He won the HundrED 2017 award as one of the global education innovators. He has launched several global educational projects like the Climate Action project, which is supported by Dalai Lama, Greenpeace and The Jane Goodall Foundation.

Acknowledgements

If it weren't for the Global Teacher Prize (GTP) and the Varkey Foundation, none of us would have met each other, let alone collaborated on a book. Mr. Sunny Varkey's vision of raising the status of the teaching profession through the Prize, and supporting the work of finalists to bring about positive change in international education systems, made this possible. His generosity knows no bounds to make sure that every child has a proper education. Vikas Pota, CEO of the Foundation, gave us the confidence to pursue our dream of making a global impact. His enthusiastic support sustained us through times when this project seemed overwhelming. Great teams often have great coaches, and Alice Cornish served that role for us. She pushed us to think deeper about issues and to examine each topic from multiple points of view. The entire Varkey team was instrumental in helping this book become a reality, especially Cate Noble, Jonathan Simons and Nicholas Piachaud. We can't thank them enough.

Klaus Schwab's book *The Fourth Industrial Revolution* inspired us to write about the role of teachers in these unprecedented times. Education is often mentioned as a solution to society's problems, but too often the perspectives on how to do this are limited and lack the critical voices of those who are implementing policy at the classroom level. We are eternally grateful to Mr. Schwab for supporting the inclusion of teacher voice in this discussion.

Andreas Schleicher's commitment to improving education is obvious to anyone who has the pleasure to meet him. As former GTP finalists, each of us has had that pleasure. Few individuals on the planet understand the intricacies and interconnectedness of international educational policy as deeply as he does. Although he is far from the classroom as Director of Education and Skills at Organisation for Economic Cooperation and Development (OECD), he is a true champion of teachers. We are deeply grateful for his support and willingness to be a part of this endeavor.

Thank you to the experts and researchers that added their voices to this book. Your guidance and knowledge has pushed us in our classrooms and have enhanced the profession.

Most importantly, this book would not be possible if it weren't for the examples of teachers doing amazing work around the globe. We were constantly inspired by our peers, especially other GTP finalists in the Varkey Teacher Ambassador network. Each of you, and millions of others around the globe who have not yet been recognized, are changing the world every day, one student at a time. We are humbled and honored to share some of your narratives, and we hope those who read will be as inspired by them as we were. Thank you for your tireless commitment to our next generation.

Lastly, we would all like to thank a few people individually.

Armand Doucet

I would never had tried to write a book if it wasn't for the confidence and support of my loving wife Nicole. She sacrifices for me to chase my dreams of trying to make the world a better place. My two beautiful girls, Audréanne and Arianne, are the reminder every day why education matters so much. Their curiosity and zest for life need to be nurtured throughout their lives. Our future is with our children; we owe it to them to do our best. Without my wife and kids cheering me on, I would not have had this chance to collaborate with this incredible team of authors.

Thank you to my parents for letting me chase my passions throughout my childhood. I owe you both an unpayable debt. I have been lucky enough to have three siblings that I try to imitate every day. My brother Pierre, you have inspired me with your courage; this book has a lot of you in it. My sister Marianne, I wish that everybody in this world could have as kind a heart as you have; thank you for your support and advice throughout this process. To my sister Lillie, you are and always will be the teacher I try to imitate in my own classroom. To my close friends, Eddie, Matt, Denny and André: thank you for keeping me sane.

Lisa Hrabluk and Wicked Ideas, thank you for pulling out all stops to put New Brunswick on the map and helping me out at every turn. This book never makes your book club without your honest help.

I would like to thank the New Brunswick Department of Education, in particular our Deputy Minister John Mclaughlin, Assistant

Deputy Minister Chris Treadwell and Director of Curriculum Kimberly Bauer for their support and advice as I tried sorting through my ideas. To the Anglophone East School District, in particular Superintendent Gregg Ingersoll. To Liz Nowlan, Mario Chiasson, Diane Gillis, Liz Nowlan and Pamela Wilson, thank you for giving me the opportunity to become a better teacher and for your incredible support.

Last but certainly not least, I would like to thank all my colleagues, past and present. They are a wonderful group of teachers who keep pushing the boundaries of what our profession will look like in the future.

Jelmer Evers

Writing, teaching, traveling. It is all time consuming. There is so much to read, and inspiration comes and goes. Staying up late, weekends away. That requires a lot of flexibility and understanding. I'd like to thank my wonderful loved ones – Ilja, for being so supportive and understanding. But also for being an inspiration in education yourself. I don't know anyone who exemplifies what we need in education as well as you. And my two boys, Finn and Syp, who have had to put up a lot from me, but are always curious of what daddy is up to now. I'm doing this for you.

My contributions to this book have been inspired by so many people. My wonderful colleagues at UniC, especially the Social Sciences Department: Rianne Neering, Hanneke van der Graaff, Margit Pothoven, Nico Jongerius and Koen Assman. What I learned by working with you has been the foundation for my thinking and writing. And of course, my students, who have to put up a lot from me. And thanks for being so understanding when I'm off to a faraway country to do "something" with education.

I'd also like to thank David Edwards and Fred van Leeuwen and all of my colleagues at Education International and national unions who are an inspiration in their leadership and activism and who have opened up my eyes in so many ways. We stand stronger together. Thank you, Dennis Shirley, Andy Hargreaves, Carol Campbell for showing us the way and for just being good friends; Dick van der Wateren for putting the alternative into practice, the hardest part; Arjan van der Meij and Per Ivar Kloen, the maker boys, who exemplify the joy and professionalism of our profession; and finally, my flip brother in arms in writing and in teaching, Rene Kneyber, for starting it all.

Elisa Guerra

Writing this book in collaboration with a team of outstanding teachers and dear friends has been one of the most rewarding experiences in my professional life. I am deeply grateful to Armand, our leader, whose vision and drive brought the team together – and the book to life. Mike was always generous with his time and expertise and, as a native speaker and seasoned writer, provided sensible feedback to my chapter. I had previously worked with Jelmer when he invited me to author a vignette for *Flip the System*, the book he edited in 2015. His professional connections and clever insights proved invaluable for the group. Koen was the tech-savvy one that powered the survey directed to the global teachers, which was so vital for my chapter, and sent me updated results and summaries every time I asked. I learned so much from Nadia, both from her book *The Bridge to Brilliance* and from the lively discussions we had in Toronto. It was uplifting – and humbling – to have the chance to interact with these incredible educators. I was on my tiptoes all the time, trying to reach to their level.

My chapter about education today was heavily influenced by the work of Professor Eduardo Andere. His extensive research on comparative education provided a framework from which I could construct the narrative. His books about learning in world-class schools were a founding stone for my writing. Dr. Andere gave detailed answers to my many questions and provided feedback for my final manuscript. I was fortunate to be able to step on the shoulders of a giant.

Lucy Crehan shared her experiences about what it is like to teach in five of the top-performing school systems in the world – her findings and anecdotes helped me spice the chapter. Gabriela Kaplan became a friend after 2 days together at a conference in Mexico City, where I learned about her role in using technology to remotely teach English to thousands of students in Uruguay.

I became a teacher out of love for my children, Leo, Annie and Santiago. They have always been my inspiration and drive. My parents, Enrique and Elisa, are unconditional supporters and guides. And my life would not be complete without Eduardo, whose love and example are helping me grow into the person I want to become.

Dr. Nadia Lopez

First and foremost, I would like to thank Armand for asking me to be a part of this revolutionary work. The process of creating the book is reflective of the skills needed to thrive within the Fourth Industrial Revolution: collaboration, critical thinking and communication. To the team at the Varkey Foundation, thank you for the opportunity to serve as a global ambassador and creating an extended family that has allowed me to learn from phenomenal teachers who embody education excellence. To my fellow Varkey Teacher Ambassadors, you are all phenomenal and make me proud to be an educator.

I must also say thank you to my family, who time and time again keep making sacrifices that have allowed me to travel the world to share my work. Cenne, you are my reason for living, and all that I do is for you. Mommy, without you, I don't know how far I would be in this world. I thank God for choosing me to be your daughter. Daddy, you have taught me the essence of resilience – thank you. Justin, Rayne and Max, I love you so much! To my scholars, because of you I get to stand on stages that I dared to dream of; I am a living example of where you can go and what you can be. Keith, Donsha, Yves, Monique and the Brooklyn Combine family, I love you for always having my back. To all of my friends and family members, thank you for your support and always lifting me up.

Michael Soskil

Teaching is the greatest profession in the world. Not only do we get to make a difference in the lives of others every day, but we get to teach the next generation how to change the world for the better. My students constantly remind me that the solutions to all of the world's problems are trapped inside the passions of our children. For their inspiration and for making my job so much fun, I thank them.

Throughout my years in education, my professional growth has been fueled by the outstanding teachers around me. During our work together, my co-authors forced me to think more deeply about education issues than I ever have before. Within Wallenpaupack, my home district and through an online professional learning network (PLN) that spans the globe, I am pushed beyond my comfort zone by the excellence of those to whom I am connected. Thank you, Patti Duncan, for starting me on this journey by teaching me the power of online collaboration. My contribution to this book would not have been possible without all those in my PLN. Many of the narratives of their amazing work are included in my chapters. Many more examples of exceptional dedication to students had to be left out due to space constraints. I am appreciative to every one of these educators, and to others around the globe I have not yet met who are having a positive impact on the world's children.

I cannot thank my family and friends enough for their support and encouragement. Marvin Soskil, Jayne Wenner, Brett Soskil, Dyane Smokorowski, Mairi Cooper, John Wenner, Wendy Feld, Jed Dearybury, Beth Heidemann and Melissa Morris are always a text or a phone call away to give me advice, talk me off an emotional ledge or proofread a paragraph. So many more than I can list offered a kind word or piece of advice at exactly the right time during the writing process. Throughout my life my mother, Marita Wenner, has been a role model showing me what it means to help others. Her example, along with the feedback she gave as I wrote, was invaluable.

Finally, and most importantly, I must thank my wife and children. Abigail and Michael, I could not be prouder of the wonderful people you have become. You are the reason for this book. My generation has a commitment to giving yours the ability to have a bright and prosperous future. I hope that my writing moves us a little closer to that goal. Lori, I love you with all my heart. Words can't express how appreciative I am of the sacrifices you make to allow me to pursue my passions. This wouldn't have been possible without your love and support.

Koen Timmers

First and foremost, I would like to thank my wife Rachel for standing beside me throughout my career and writing this book. She has been my inspiration and motivation for continuing to improve my knowledge and move my career forward. She is my rock, and I dedicate my chapter to her. I also thank my wonderful son, Mauro, for always making me smile and for understanding those moments when I was writing this book and spending time on setting up global educational projects instead of playing games. I hope that one day, he can read this book and understand why I spent so much time in front of my computer.

I'd like to thank my parents for allowing me to follow my ambitions and passions throughout my childhood.

I also want to thank PXL-education Hasselt, CVO de Verdieping, executives Marc, Wouter, Maddy and colleagues for supporting me to push boundaries in my classroom.

No global initiatives happen without strong connections and communities. I'd like to thank my global friends and PLN in the Microsoft in Education, Varkey Teacher Ambassador, MTGS and NNSTOY communities. Also, my co-authors inspired me a lot and offered a helping hand throughout the writing process. They pushed me to go further for which I want to thank them.

Last but not least, I'd like to thank the Kakuma ambassadors and Climate Action participants like Paula, Kaylyn, Jim, Emma, Kelli, Susanna, Angels et al. for willing to step outside their comfort zone, for allowing their students to have great experiences and for exchanging their best practices and anecdotes, which partly helped to shape this book. True success in education is built on a foundation of caring educators willing to bring change and innovation into their classrooms at the right moment. I also want to thank PXL-education Hasselt, CVO de Verdieping, executives Ben Lambrechts, Marc Hermans, Wouter Hustinx, Maddy Lecok and colleagues for supporting me to push boundaries in my classroom.

Introduction

Armand Doucet and Jelmer Evers

The six of us from all over the globe were sitting in a room in Toronto at the beginning of what turned out to be a very intense 2-day session, where we explored the state of the world and the future of education. As we were just settling in, the question "Why are we here?" came up. Why are we here writing this book? As we each took our turn, a pattern emerged. Each of us basically answered, "For our children." We are not only teachers, but parents as well. We are also profoundly worried about the current state of the world in which our children will grow up. One by one, we listed all the challenges we saw around us: devastating climate change, endemic inequity, rising inequality, populism and authoritarianism, and the resulting risk of conflict. What can education achieve? How should it change? What is our role in this as teachers?

It wasn't just an academic conversation. These global challenges reflect real problems from our everyday practice in our classrooms. These also reflect the hopes and fears of our students as they too struggle with what the future will hold for them. We all teach in very different settings. Mike Soskil and Nadia Lopez both hail from the United States for example, but one teaches in a conservative rural setting, whilst the other is a principal in a deprived urban area. But even when we do teach in more affluent environments, we all know that every student brings their whole being into the classroom and that the world – whether it be local or global – always influences and changes how they feel, act and think. Each individual student is a new independent and constantly changing variable in an ever-changing context. This nuance often gets lost when education is discussed, especially at the global policy level.

"First, we wanted to write this book for our children. Second, we wanted to get our teachers' voice heard." Emphasizing the nuances of our everyday practice. We are not academics, but practitioners. We are however academically qualified, inclined and evidence informed. This book, though, is not a research study, but it is a reflection of our experiences and the experiences of many of our colleagues. Those experiences, though, are backed up by a wealth of research and knowledge of the world. Teachers exemplify three important Aristotelian virtues: *Episteme, Techne,* and *Phronesis. Episteme* is the knowledge of universal truth (science), and *Techne* is the ability to make things. But what Aristotle regarded as the highest intellectual virtue – and what captures the teaching profession best – was what he called *Phronesis,* practical wisdom.[1] We need wisdom to make judgements about what is desirable or good again and again. To say it in more popular terms: we need more practical knowledge in education, and we want to strengthen that voice with this book.

Between the six of us, we already knew so many inspirational examples of teachers making a difference worldwide. So, while the state of the world sometimes gives us reason for despair, stories about empowered students and inspiring teaching give us hope. In that room in Toronto, we were experiencing a feeling of standing at the precipice – a fork in the road – where we sensed that the teaching profession could be crucial in leading the way forward. The teaching profession possesses those traits and moral purpose that might be an inspiration for other segments of society.

There has been a wealth of literature on the extraordinary era of change we are experiencing. The book that started us on this road was *The Fourth Industrial Revolution* by Klaus Schwab, Founder and Executive Chairman of the World Economic Forum (WEF).[2] The main thesis of the book is that we are living in a time of unprecedented change, a Fourth Industrial Revolution driven by new technologies. Automation and globalization have already profoundly changed global society from the 1980s onwards, and these changes are now happening exponentially. We are indeed standing at the precipice. And whether we are up to the task to deal with these challenges remains to be seen, according to Schwab. But he is optimistic.

Our book takes us on a dazzling tour, looking at a wide array of technological breakthroughs and possibilities. The difference with the

1 Biesta, G. (2007, February). Why 'What Works' Won't Work: Evidence-Based Practice and the Democratic Deficit in Educational Research. *Educational Theory,* 57(1): 1–22. doi: 10.1111/j.1741–5446.2006.00241.x.

2 Schwab, K. (2017). *The Fourth Industrial Revolution.* UK: Penguin.

previous revolutions is that this one combines the physical, digital and biological worlds. Schwab identifies 21 deep shifts, citing examples like Implantable Technologies, Big Data, Artificial Intelligence (AI), Robotics, 3D-Printing, Neurotechnologies and Designer Beings. Some of these are already having a big impact on our society, indeed, on us personally. The six of us writing this book wouldn't be where we were, sitting in that room in Toronto, if we hadn't embraced some of these technological changes, which we will explore further in our chapters. But Schwab rightfully addresses the positive and negative sides of these technological changes. For example, Big Data and AI might enable us to make better and faster decisions, but there are also increasing worries about privacy, existing biases, accountability and trust. Are algorithms really as neutral as they are portrayed to be?

Since the publication of *The Fourth Industrial Revolution*, things haven't improved. It is increasingly clear that globalization and automation are linked to the political, economic and social problems we are facing today.[3] Where the world should be coming together, it is becoming more authoritarian, not more democratic. We are living in an era of *democratic recession* which increasingly is starting to resemble the 1930s.[4] According to *Freedom House*'s annual report – in 2017 ominously titled *Populists and Autocrats: The Dual Threat to Global Democracy* – 2016 was the 11th year of consecutive decline in global freedom.[5] Where we should be fighting inequality and inequity, these gaps have only widened. Allegedly, the richest 62 people of the world now own more than the bottom 50 per cent of the world population.[6] And although the Paris climate accords were a monumental historical achievement, the question remains to be seen if we can follow up on the commitment. The International Monetary Fund in its World Economic Outlook 2017 reported that with the current scenarios, the poorest countries will be hit hardest by climate change.[7]

3 Rodrik, D. (2017, June 15). Populism and the Economics of Globalization. *Draft.* Cambridge.
4 Wolf, M. (2017, September 19). Democracy and Capitalism: The Odd Couple. *Financial Times.*
5 Puddington, A., & Roylance, T. (2017). *Populists and Autocrats: The Dual Threat to Global Democracy: Freedom in the World 2017.* London: Freedom House.
6 Hardoon, D. (2017). *An Economy for the 99%: It's Time to Build a Human Economy That Benefits Everyone, Not Just the Privileged Few.* Oxford: Oxfam International.
7 International Monetary Fund. (2017, October 2). *World Economic Outlook 2017: Seeking Sustainable Growth Short-Term Recovery, Long-Term Challenges.* Washington: IMF.

As Klaus Schwab rightly says, we need to build new institutions, new governance, new networks and new leadership that foster trust and can create sustainable change in our societies. Crucially, we need to evaluate new ways to educate our children: "In the end, it comes down to people, culture and values." He identifies four different types of intelligences that he sees as crucial in overcoming the enormous challenges ahead:

> **Contextual (the mind) intelligence** is about how we understand and apply our knowledge. Solutions to 'wicked problems' like climate change "require collaboration across boundaries with leaders from business, government, civil society, faith, and academia." **Emotional (the heart) intelligence** is about "how we process and integrate our thoughts and feelings and relate to ourselves and to one another. Skills like self-awareness, self-regulation, motivation, empathy and social skills are essential." **Inspired (the soul) intelligence** is about "how we use a sense of individual and shared purpose, trust, and other virtues to effect change and act towards the common good." **Physical (the body) intelligence** is about how "we cultivate and maintain our personal health and well-being and that of those around us to be in a position to apply the energy required for both individual and systems transformation."

And of course, there is much hope to be found. As the late Hans Rossling never tired of pointing out in his presentations, the world has seen tremendous progress. More than half of the world's' population has risen out of poverty. Recently, nations of the world created a roadmap to a sustainable future at the 2015 World Education Forum, hosted by the Republic of Korea. Of the 17 Sustainable Development Goals (SDG), Education (SDG4) was specifically mentioned as a foundation for change. Between 19 and 22 May 2015, over 1,600 participants from 160 countries, including over 120 ministers, heads and members of delegations, heads of agencies and officials of multilateral and bilateral organizations, and representatives of civil society, the teaching profession, youth and the private sector, adopted the Incheon Declaration for Education 2030 where SDG4 was further specified. In September 2015, all Sustainable Development Goals were adopted at an in historic meeting at the United Nations (UN).

But we still have a very steep uphill climb ahead of us. According to the latest figures in 2015 by the United Nations Educational, Scientific and Cultural Organization (UNESCO), there are 264 million primary- and secondary-age children and youth out of school. Less than one in five countries guarantee 12 years of free and compulsory education. Only 66 per cent of countries have achieved gender parity – an equal number of girls and boys – in primary education, 45 per cent in lower secondary and 25 per cent in upper secondary. Between 2009 and 2012, only 7 per cent of teacher education programs covered education for sustainable development.

The education share of total aid for the Global South fell for six consecutive years, from 10 per cent in 2009 to 6.9 per cent in 2015. Education was more exposed to the risk of corruption than even the construction industry in the European Union in the period 2009–2014. These are just some of the facts showing a light on the enormity of the challenge ahead.

Too often, education by itself is seen as the answer to all these challenges. We have lost count how many times we've seen bridging the "skills gap" in an automated future as the *deus ex machina* to these challenges. Just like technology, education isn't the solution to all our political, social and economic challenges. It does have a crucial part to play though.

This challenge calls for a holistic view of education. We need to look at not only what happens in the classroom, but also how we design our educational system. Renowned scholar Dennis Shirley has laid down the need for this in his book *The New Imperatives for Educational Change*.[8] In it, he offers five old and five new imperatives for educational change. The old ones will sound familiar to many teachers, we have felt the brunt of these forces in our classroom.

Here then, are the old imperatives. The *ideological imperative* that emphasized market competition, testing and standardization as levers to improve schools – despite the absence of evidence to support these directions; the *imperial imperative* that projected this ideology onto other schools and systems as the best way to move forward, even when those other systems were already succeeding by employing different ways to organize their work; the *prescriptive imperative* that mandated the daily work of educators from higher levels of school bureaucracies; the *insular imperative* that overloaded educators with so many policy demands that their ability to learn from other schools and systems has been seriously impeded; the *instrumental imperative* that denied students and teachers in relation to their economic contributions, with a concomitant disregard for values of compassion, solidarity or service.

8 Shirley, D. (2017). *The New Imperatives of Educational Change*. New York: Routledge.

Shirley proposes five new imperatives which should guide a new wave of educational change. Again, these will ring true to many teachers. The *evidentiary imperative*: collaboration, trust and professionalism are key to high achievement. The *interpretive imperative*: we should not discard data and evidence, but it must engage with evidence on all levels. Policies and practice must always be contextual and engage the profession and the public. The *professional imperative*: instead of teachers having to do as they are told, they have to be professionals who are able to make judgements. The *global imperative*: instead of the teacher being alone in the classroom, we have to strive for global learning in education. Finally, the *existential imperative*: what is education for? We need to educate the whole child and provide a holistic curriculum and experience.

Just like Klaus Schwab, Dennis Shirley talks about the promise of the present moment. There is reason for hope and optimism. All across the world, teachers are finding new ways to ensure that their students receive an education that prepares them for the Fourth Industrial Revolution. Not only in the classroom, but also outside of it. Whilst we have tried to be comprehensive, this book is not meant to be exhaustive. We've tried to find our voice and bring our experiences to bear around topics that we as teachers think are important. The chapters have an individual voice, but are a collective effort, as we all contributed to each other's chapters.

In Chapter 1, "Education in a time of unprecedented change," Michael addresses the challenges we face in a world rapidly changing due to technology. He stresses the need for the best parts of humanity and empathy to remain at the core of our education systems, and focuses on the importance of teachers in making this happen.

In Chapter 2, "Education today: a collection of snapshots," Elisa, rather than trying to explain education today from a single perspective, will present a collection of snapshots, taken from different narratives and research data. We will hear the voices of teachers and experts from around the world as they try to frame education at the threshold of the Fourth Industrial Revolution.

In Chapter 3, "Overcoming equity gaps in and through education," Michael describes the dangers of inequity inside and outside our schools and examines ways to help close those gaps. He explains how, by using data well and looking at qualitative narratives that show the lived experiences of marginalized populations, we can scale great teaching practices will help move our society in the right direction.

In Chapter 4, "Teach ME: the learner profile," Armand will provide teachers with an overview of core knowledge, literacies, competencies and character for the Fourth Industrial Revolution classroom and a practical guide to introducing this holistic approach.

In Chapter 5, "The power of learning," Nadia takes us on her journey to give us insight on how we get teachers ready for the Fourth Industrial Revolution and educate teachers for Dennis Shirley's New Imperatives for Educational Change. Teachers, she argues, must be lifelong learners.

In Chapter 6, "Contextualizing personalization in education," Armand will explore the rise of personalized education, and he will provide a practical template from classrooms around the world on how to proceed down this path in an ethical manner.

In Chapter 7, "Evolution of technology in the classroom," Koen shares with us how he became one of the most innovative teachers in the world. His examples, as well as many from his peers around the world, showcase that great pedagogy with a proper use of technology can enhance the learning experience.

In Chapter 8, "Flip the system," Jelmer will discuss systemic change. He will explain how, by flipping the system, we can change education from the ground up. That will take professionalism and also activism by teachers to help build those new systems. We need to embrace a new paradigm: the networked teacher.

You will find that the six of us agree on many things and disagree on others. Each of us brings a different perspective to the discussion of education in the Fourth Industrial Revolution. During our work on this book, there were disagreements – often heated and intense, but always respectful. Through the process, each of us has grown as individuals and professionals. This mirrors education. It is complex, messy and beautiful. Passionate teachers having professional discussions about what is best for kids leads to a better education system. We hope that this book leads to positive change, while serving as a catalyst for others to have necessary complex conversations. We are standing at the precipice. The future is unknown. Each of us has shared our most passionate ideas on education, channeling our experiences and the voices of inspiring educators from around the world. Individually, each of these chapters offers a path forward. Collectively, they offer a vision of how education can lead us through an unknown future to a place of peace and prosperity.

Chapter I

Education in a Time of Unprecedented Change

Michael Soskil

As I walked through the village in the Maasai Mara National Reserve asking questions about traditional education for his people, my host stressed the importance the community placed on their children. The Maasai people are regarded as Africa's greatest warriors. They live in circular villages in the savanna, using their famed swords to protect their families and livestock from lions. For generations, their traditional greeting has reflected their core values. One Maasai meeting another, whether the strongest and fiercest warrior or the eldest grandmother, would ask, "Kasserian Ingera?" which translates to "How are the children?" The traditional and hoped-for response is, "All the children are well." The Maasai understand that societal health is dependent upon the wellbeing of all the children.

All of our children are not well. In our global society, too many of our children are living in poverty. Too many of our children do not have access to food or clean drinking water. Too many of our children are living with the consequences of conflict and war. While many organizations and individuals are working to ensure the health of our next generation, collectively, we have prioritized other goals and have put our future in jeopardy. Many of our children are not well because we have been more focused in our education systems on what is easily quantified rather than what is most important. We have lost sight of what our children need to be happy, healthy, and contributing citizens to the global society they will inherit from us.

Education is one of the most fundamental human acts. From the time that humans developed the capacity to communicate, older generations have passed knowledge on to their successors, carefully sharing the most important aspects of who we are. Our ability to feel and empathize defines us as a species, and it is no coincidence that the part of our brain that evolved to control memory is also responsible for supporting our emotions.[1] Because teachers represent the most important relationship to students in schools, and human relationships are essential to learning, the excellence of our education system will never reach beyond the caliber of the educators within it. Outstanding education systems are filled with outstanding schools. Outstanding schools are made so because they are filled with outstanding teachers.

The backbone of our society is education. All around the globe from the most affluent cities to the most isolated rural villages, schools are the center of the community. Societal health is dependent upon our ability to pass skills necessary for survival to our future generations. Each community has different educational needs and challenges that must be addressed, but every society's success is dependent upon its ability to maintain an educated populace over time. Our future hinges on the learning and wellbeing of our children.

The New World of Learning

We are now entering an unprecedented time in human history. Increasing computer power along with nearly ubiquitous Internet connectivity will change the way humans live, work, interact and relate to each other. As we mentioned in the Introduction, Klaus Schwab, founder and executive chairman of the World Economic Forum, describes this period of expansive digitization and automation as "The Fourth Industrial Revolution." As Artificial Intelligence (AI) and machine learning, the "Internet of Things," biotechnological advances, and nanotechnology turn the most imaginative science fiction into reality, we will be forced to continually reevaluate the question, "What does it mean to be human?"

This increased digitization and automation have significantly impacted education in recent years. Content delivery is increasingly accessed online. The Khan Academy was started in 2004 when Salmon Khan started recording tutorial videos for his cousins and posting them on the Internet. As others discovered the benefits of learning through online videos, Khan developed more content to meet the demand. The non-profit service has expanded to become the flag bearer for online educational content with more than 40 million students and 2 million teachers

---

1 Catani, M., Dell'acqua, F. & Thiebaut, M. (2013, September). A Revised Limbic System Model for Memory, Emotion and Behavior. Retrieved November 5, 2017, from www.ncbi.nlm.nih.gov/pubmed/23850593

using the website every month. Anyone wishing to learn about a topic can probably find dozens of relevant videos on YouTube. In 2016, 58 million people took Massive Open Online Courses (MOOCs) offered by over 700 different universities.[2] Knowledge is more easily available, cheaper to access, and more easily curated than ever before in human history.

At the same time, the importance of understanding how knowledge in different disciplines connects, understanding the applications of knowledge to solve complex problems and grasping the ethical implications of those applications is more valuable than ever before. As the Internet age made information ubiquitous, the workforce began to transition toward a focus on "21st Century Skills" such as critical thinking, creativity, communication and the ability to collaborate with others. Now, in the Fourth Industrial Revolution, a further transition is taking place. As the communication between computers and AI increases, information will be shared without humans. That digital transfer of information between devices, combined with advances in the capabilities of AI, will lead to the automation of any job that can be represented by a series of algorithms. We've already seen this trend start to take place.

In 1996, someone hired to drive a truck of goods from farmland to the city would have needed to be very knowledgeable about the roads he or she would have to drive. If a road was unexpectedly closed, a new route would have to be used. Drivers who knew the geography of their area well were able to reroute without taking time to stop their truck to look at paper maps. This saved time and money.

By 2006, GPS systems and crowdsourced traffic mapping by Waze, an app for mobile devices, made paper maps obsolete. Truck drivers no longer needed to be geography experts to efficiently navigate around obstacles. Ten years later in 2016, self-driving Uber cars began driving passengers around Pittsburgh, Pennsylvania. Within a decade, it is very possible that truck drivers will cease to exist. The trucks, loaded by machines rather than humans, will drive themselves.

An education system that does not address this trend is irrelevant. An education system unable to adapt to the speed of innovation in society is obsolete. An education system that is not preparing citizens to be happy and healthy in the world they will live is worthless.

2 By the Numbers: MOOCS in 2016 – Class Central. (2017, January 8). Retrieved November 5, 2017, from www.class-central.com/report/mooc-stats-2016/

I graduated university and started teaching in 1997, 20 years before this book was written and just a few years after the World Wide Web began to be widely used. My first experience with the Internet was accessing information using the University of Minnesota's Gopher Protocol, a precursor to the Internet we know today. Being able to send an email or access a weather report on a monochrome screen seemed groundbreaking at the time. I didn't even mind walking a kilometer across the university campus or waiting my turn to use one of the shared computers in the library. At that time, research was still mostly done by looking at old journal articles on microfilm or microfiche. It was both difficult to find relevant information and extremely time consuming.

In my wildest dreams, I could not have imagined what teaching would be like now, when the entirety of human knowledge is accessible through a device in my pocket. I regularly have live video conversations with people around the globe. Tools like Skype Translator and Google Pixel Buds make it possible to have those conversations with those who do not even speak the same language. With Moore's Law telling us that processing power doubles every 18 months and with quantum computing on the horizon, it is clear that the changes in the last third of my career will be far greater than those in my first 20 years.

The same technology that is changing my job as a teacher is giving my students the opportunity to become empowered problem solvers. They collaborate with children across the planet on projects to overcome inequities they identify. In the past 4 years, they have interviewed scientists in Antarctica, learned from astronauts on the International Space Station, and collaborated with people in over 90 countries. Each connection allows them to share a little of our community and themselves with the world and to internalize transformational experiences that only come with being exposed to different cultures. My students have read books on natural resources to Ukrainian kids, discussed gender equity in STEM careers with peers in Tunisia and partnered with classes around the globe to tackle some of the world's biggest problems.

Each new exciting learning experience that is available to my students brings with it new questions. Am I preparing them for the future they will face? Am I giving them the skills they need to face the problems with which our generation is leaving them? How do I continue to meet the demands of my job and also stay current with the rapidly changing world outside our school's walls?

Perhaps most importantly, I am forced to ask myself if I am preparing students for the ethical challenges they will face in this new world.

In his 2013 New York Times article titled "The Perils of Perfection," Evgeny Morozov details the pitfalls we face as a society when technology is used to solve problems for economic gain without regard to the humanistic threats the solutions would pose to society.[3] It might seem like an incredible advancement to be able to implant a chip into an individual's brain that gives them instant access to all the information available on Wikipedia. But, what do we do if such a chip gets hacked? It will be wonderful to cure diseases like cancer and heart disease, but how are we going to deal with issues of overpopulation and resource scarcity that will ensue? Globalization, driven by technology, is reshaping the human experience. Digital applications that eliminate memory loss, medical advancements that allow for the genetic altering of unborn children, and programs that allow social media accounts to posthumously communicate on our behalf using algorithms to determine what we probably would have posted – all could be possible in the near future. Each advancement comes with ethical strings that threaten our human identity.

In 2006, in the midst of the Internet age, Ruben Puentedura developed the SAMR model to direct technology integration in schools. SAMR is an acronym for Substitution, Augmentation, Modification and Redefinition. The model guides educators from using technology to simply replace analog lessons toward innovative uses toward innovative uses of digital tools. For Puentedura, "redefinition" is the highest form of educational technology utilization in schools. He explains it as, "using technology to create completely new tasks, previously inconceivable."[4]

Many schools and educational systems are still using SAMR to drive their technology integration. Many more have still yet to embrace technology as a necessary part of the learning experience. Yet, SAMR is already insufficient to describe the technology integration to which we should be aspiring in this complex time.

With the world we live in being constantly transformed by previously unimaginable advances and the ethical dilemmas that come with them, educational redefinition must evolve where technology is used beyond the creation of new learning experiences (Figure 1.1).

3 Ltd, B. C. (n.d.). Retrieved November 5, 2017, from www.befrienders.org/suicide-statistics
4 Catani, M., Dell'acqua, F., & Thiebaut, M. (2013, September). A Revised Limbic System Model for Memory, Emotion and Behavior. Retrieved November 5, 2017, from www.ncbi.nlm.nih.gov/pubmed/23850593

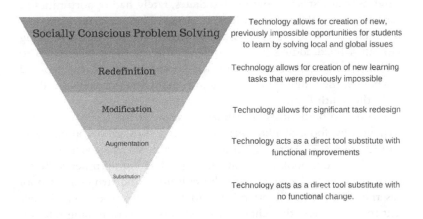

Figure 1.1 SAMR model adapted for the Fourth Industrial Revolution

If education is to keep pace with the Fourth Industrial Revolution outside of our schools, it must empower our next generation to be both solutionary and socially conscious. Learning must be seen as a vehicle for creating solutions to issues that threaten the health of our global society at the local, national and international levels. Much of the content we teach in schools has a practical application to help our fellow humans. Students should not have to wait until graduation to experience the relevance of their learning.

Fernando Reimers, Director of the Global Education Innovation Initiative and International Education Policy Program at Harvard University believes that the current landscape of our global society requires us to focus on pedagogies that empower students. "Education," he claims, "should cultivate the agency, voice and efficacy of people. We need to help learners develop the ability to use what they know to solve problems."[5]

When Stephen Ritz left a box of vegetable seeds behind the radiator in his classroom in the Bronx Borough of New York City, he had no idea that the trajectory of his teaching career and his school community was about to drastically change. As the seeds grew, so did his students' curiosity. Children in his area, both the poorest and hungriest

5 Fernando Reimers. (n.d.). Retrieved November 1, 2017, from www.thefivethings.org/fernando-reimers/

congressional district in the United States, rarely had opportunities to learn about healthy food and how it grows. The urban environment, in which almost 50 per cent of his students were homeless and living without a fixed address, was devoid of farms, gardens and places to buy fresh produce. Areas like this are known as "food deserts," and nowhere in the United States are there as many hungry people as there are in the South Bronx.[6]

In order to both satisfy his student's curiosity and to provide them with healthy food, Stephen began teaching through aeroponic gardening. Instead of learning about photosynthesis and other required curriculum from books, his students began learning in order to better grow crops in the school. Soon the culture of the struggling school was transformed. Daily attendance in the school rose from 40 per cent to 93 per cent, the school achieved 100 per cent passing rates on standardized tests, and 2,200 jobs that supported the initiative were created in the community that allowed families another source of income. Students began bringing home fresh vegetables to their families, which made children healthier and more able to learn when they came to school. Stephen's work led to the creation of Green Bronx Machine, a non-profit organization which helps schools and communities across the planet teach children through gardening. Every one of the students learning through these programs knows exactly why they are learning. The connection to life is obvious.

While utilizing engaging pedagogies and new advancements in schools as tools to develop critical thinkers staves off irrelevance, by focusing exclusively on technology we risk losing sight of the very reason we educate students in the first place. With innovations continually opening new opportunities for students, we cannot forget our moral obligation to the next generation to provide the skills and qualities they need to navigate the world they will inherit. Empathy, the uniquely human character trait that is also most predictive of success in life,[7] must be at the heart of how we prepare our next generation for their future.

The noblest use of technology in schools is to provide students with the opportunity to learn while developing innovative solutions

6 McMillan, T. & Photographs by Kitra Cahana, Stephanie Sinclair, and Amy Toensing. (n.d.). The New Face of Hunger. Retrieved November 5, 2017, from www.nationalgeographic.com/foodfeatures/hunger/
7 (n.d.). Retrieved October 20, 2017, from www.eiconsortium.org/reports/jj_ei_study.html

to problems being created by unintended consequences of the Fourth Industrial Revolution. Combining foundational knowledge in new ways, working through the design process, and solving pressing societal problems provides students both the skills and competencies needed to navigate their uncertain futures. We need to nurture a generation of social innovators who will have the skills needed to overcome the significant challenges with which advancing technology will present them.

The Power of Empathy

Only by keeping education rooted in human relationships and empathy can we meet the great challenges on the horizon.

We know that our students are craving the opportunity to make a difference and shape the planet they will inherit from us. In 2017, the Varkey Foundation surveyed 20,000 young people from 20 different countries around the globe.[8] These members of "Generation Z," who were born around the turn of the millennium, shared their thoughts on education, global citizenship, issues facing our planet right now and the hopes they have for the future. Over two-thirds of the respondents indicated that making a wider contribution to our global society was something important to them. In 14 of the 20 countries, the greatest obstacle to achieving this goal was listed as a lack of knowledge about how to get involved and make a difference. Clearly, we must provide youngsters with an understanding of their power to effect positive change on their local, national, and global communities and opportunities to practice these skills.

In India, Bijal Damani of Rajkot realized the importance of connecting required curriculum with opportunities for students to have a positive impact on their community. The 11th and 12th grade class she inherited when she started teaching at the S. N. Kansanga School was notorious for behaviour issues and lack of buy-in from students. In order to show students the importance of the content they were learning, illuminate the power each of them had to make the world a better place and pass them the skills they would need to be successful in their unknown futures, Bijal helped them use their learning to create a bazaar to raise money for disadvantaged children. In

8 Varkey Foundation. (2017). Generation Z:Global Citizenship Survey. Retrieved October 14, 2017, from www.varkeyfoundation.org/generation-z-global-citizenship-survey

time, that student-run bazaar expanded to raise the equivalent of over US$ 120,000 and help over 1,800 underprivileged children per year.[9,10] This number is staggering considering India's annual median per capita income is less than US$ 1,000.[11]

There was incredible benefit for the disadvantaged children that were helped by the funds Bijal's students raised. Her students also benefitted greatly. The entrepreneurial skills they learned helped many become successful after graduation, while the compassion they practiced helped them understand the importance of respecting others as they pursued their own success. Many are now executives and employees at successful businesses, and others have started their own companies. What makes Bijal most proud, though, is that many continue to sponsor the education of underprivileged children outside of school in their own capacities. With the World Economic Forum finding that Emotional Intelligence will be one of the ten most important skills in the workforce of the near future, the benefits of this combination of service and content are obvious.

My own students have also learned how powerful their learning can be if it is used to help others and strengthen our global community. A year ago, my fifth graders were troubled as we finished a Skype call with children and their teacher in Mukuyuni, a rural village in western Kenya. During the call, the Kenyans took my students on a tour of their area, including views of a dilapidated and dangerous bridge made of logs that crossed a raging stream. They explained that some of the younger children in the village were not allowed to go to school because crossing the bridge was too treacherous. During the rainy season, no students could cross, halting their education.

After the call ended, I heard "magic" words from my students. They are magic because they tell me that my students are engaged and have identified a problem in the world that they are passionate about solving.

"Mr. Soskil, we need to do something about that."

9   Bijal Damani: Rajkot's Good Samaritan. (n.d.). Retrieved November 5, 2017, from www.forbesindia.com/article/philanthropy-awards-2014/bijal-damani-rajkots-good-samaritan/39271/1
10 Interview with Bijal Damani [Email interview]. (2017, September 24).
11 Reporter, B. (2013, December 16). India's Median Per Capita Income Lowest among BRICS: Gallup. Retrieved November 5, 2017, from www.business-standard.com/article/economy-policy/india-s-median-per-capita-income-lowest-among-brics-gallup-113121600968_1.html

The next few days were a whirlwind of research. The Kenyan teacher sent us measurements of the area. Enthusiasm built as students started learning about different bridge designs and how loads were distributed. Using concepts from math class to draw scaled plans, my students looked up materials available in that area of the world. The complexity of the issue gave a pathway for each student to connect learning to a personal passion; empathy for their peers on the other side of the world drove them to stay engaged. There was tangible excitement as students continually talked about their drive to help their new friends.

For the next month, children in my classes ideated and prototyped solutions to the bridge problem. Strongly focused on the design process, small teams of students constructed paper bridge models and used pennies to apply weight and force structural failure. Next, they tested designs with cardboard and heavier weights. Learning from the failure of each model, they engineered increasingly better designs. I would set time aside during classes to bring all the teams together so they could share the lessons they had learned with each other.

After students felt confident in their models, I had them draw scaled plans on graph paper. They spent time debating merits of each solution and voted for the best. Their choice was sent to an engineer in Kenya, who took their plans under consideration as he developed professional blueprints for a new bridge.

By the end of the school year, they had sent their design to a builder in Kenya, raised enough money to pay for the construction of the new bridge and celebrated with their friends on the other side of the world who could now get to school safely.

For both the Indian children and my own, students came to understand the intrinsic joy that comes with using learning to solve problems and make life better for others. At a time when global suicide rates are rising,[12] teens are reporting decreased happiness with their life as they get older,[13] and 20 per cent of young people in Organisation for Economic Cooperation and Development (OECD) countries will leave school before obtaining an upper secondary education,[14] provid-

---

12 Weissbourd, Rick (2003). Moral Teachers, Moral Students. Retrieved November 5, 2017, from www.ascd.org/publications/educational-leadership/mar03/vol60/num06/Moral-Teachers,-Moral-Students.aspx

13 Varkey Foundation. (2017). Generation Z: Global Citizenship Survey. Retrieved October 14, 2017, from www.varkeyfoundation.org/generation-z-global-citizenship-survey

14 O. (2017, September 12). Indicator A2 Who Is Expected to Graduate from Upper Secondary Education? Retrieved November 5, 2017, from www.oecd-ilibrary.org/education/

ing students opportunities to use learning for altruistic purposes is vital. Helping those around us feeds our soul. According to Davidson and Schuyler, "this type of behavior could result in a feedback loop, where pro-social behavior increases well-being, which then results in more pro-social behavior."[15] The more we give our children the opportunity to do good for others, the more they will feel the value of such actions, and the more they will seek out ways to do more good.

Inserting education into that feedback loop provides us with a sustainable model for learning in 2030 and beyond. When students understand the value and power of leveraging available resources for social innovation, they feel good about their education and they want more of it. This drives them to seek out new and innovative ways to learn and use knowledge to create solutions to help others. The cycle provides for the development of necessary skills, the acquisition of knowledge and the emotional intelligence our students need to navigate their future.

Education is the key to avoiding disaster. Schools must evolve to become places where experiences like the ones above become the norm. Never before have dystopian futures predicted by so many 20th century science fiction writers been more plausible. Dr. Stephen Hawking, perhaps the greatest mind of our time, predicted that our species has less than 100 years to populate a new planet if it is to survive.[16] He cited population growth and climate change, both issues being driven by technological advancements, among the reasons for his statement. Dr. Hawking also warned: "Once humans develop Artificial Intelligence, it will take off on its own and redesign itself at an ever-increasing rate. Humans, who are limited by slow biological evolution, couldn't compete and would be superseded."[17] This statement seems unfortunately prescient with Facebook recently shutting down an AI they created because they began to lose control of it.[18]

education-at-a-glance-2017/indicator-a2-who-is-expected-to-graduate-from-upper-secondary-education_eag-2017–8–en

15 Helliwell, J. F., Layard, R. & Sachs, J., eds. (2015). *World Happiness Report 2015*. New York: Sustainable Development Solutions Network.

16 Stephen Hawking: We Have 100 Years to Colonize New Planet. (n.d.). Retrieved November 5, 2017, from www.time.com/4767595/stephen-hawking-100-years-new-planet/

17 Holley, P. (2017, May 8). Stephen Hawking Now Says Humanity Has Only about 100 Years to Escape Earth. Retrieved November 5, 2017, from www.chicagotribune.com/news/nationworld/science/ct-stephen-hawking-escape-earth-20170505-story.html

18 Field, M. (2017, August 1). Facebook Shuts Down Robots after They Invent Their Own Language. Retrieved November 5, 2017, from www.telegraph.co.uk/technology/2017/08/01/facebook-shuts-robots-invent-language/

Our education systems need to become nimble enough to adapt to rapid changes, relevant enough to deal with modern technological advances, individualized enough to allow each child the opportunity to develop his or her unique skillset, and broad enough to prepare students for the global challenges they will face. Most importantly, however, for our increasingly global and digitized society to thrive, there has never been a more pressing need for us to respect, appreciate and care for each other.

The Need for Nuance in a Complex World

Complex problems demand locally relevant nuanced solutions. While the rigidity and content focus of our current education systems often stifles creative solutions, there are many excellent examples of innovative teachers and schools leveraging the tools of today's world to meet the challenges we face.

Students at the Cheery Children Education Center (CCEC) in the Kibera slum of Nairobi come from abject poverty in the largest slum in Africa. This hasn't stopped school director Jairus Makambi and head teacher Emmily Minayo from giving children the opportunity to develop into globally aware world changers. Starting with one laptop and an Internet connection about 5 years ago, the school of about 300 students began connecting with other classes and content experts via Internet videoconference. Children who had never seen the ocean or been outside the slum began learning from shark experts in the Bahamas, interviewing NASA astronauts about their time in space and participating in cultural exchanges with classrooms around the world. Instead of feeling disadvantaged by their situation, the CCEC staff helped the children understand the power of being educated and sharing knowledge with others. The students began offering live lessons on their culture, language, and music to other children over the Internet. My own students participated in a learning exchange with CCEC students in which recorded videos were sent to us each week teaching the Swahili language in exchange for videos my students created teaching mathematics with materials we had in our school.

Just as we see innovation develop at breakneck speed outside schools, innovation in education tends to snowball. This was certainly the case at the Cheery school. As the students began to grow into their role as global citizens, the school gained worldwide recognition, and the staff began to build relationships with educators around the globe. Children from other continents who had developed friendships with the

CCEC students developed their own projects to help their new friends overcome some of the many dangers they faced in Kibera. Project L.I.N.C., a collaboration between youngsters in Trikala, Greece; Andover, Kansas; and my own school district in northeastern Pennsylvania, developed after kids who had connected with CCEC learned how children in the slum often became ill due to cholera and other waterborne diseases. Students in the three locations helped raise money to provide water filters for the school and for CCEC families.

This exemplifies the wonderful possibilities for our future society if it is rooted in empathetic and innovative solutionism. There is room for great optimism if technology is combined with education based in human relationships and empathy (Figure 1.2). With so many of our current world conflicts based in fear of those from different cultures and with different beliefs, education can only be the cure if we keep it connected to the best aspects of humanity.

For me, this became strikingly obvious during the most powerful moment of my teaching career. I had traveled to Kenya through a grant I obtained to document the learning exchanges my students had done with the Cheery school in the Kibera slum and to deliver the water filters purchased through Project L.I.N.C. On the day the filters were delivered, I used the one laptop at CCEC to set up a group videoconference connecting the schools who had raised money for the filters to

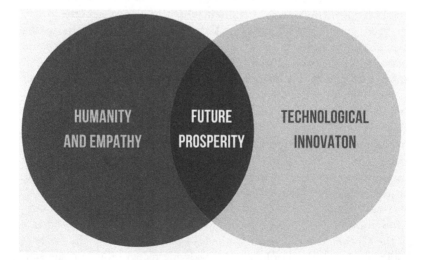

HUMANITY AND EMPATHY   FUTURE PROSPERITY   TECHNOLOGICAL INNOVATON

Figure 1.2

the children who received them. Hundreds of students from the school packed the small outdoor courtyard and crammed to see the small screen. As the filters were distributed to children to take home, euphoria spread throughout the school. During my time in Kibera, there was a cholera outbreak in the slum that killed 12 children. Students were hugging their filters, realizing that they no longer had to worry about the safety of themselves or their family members in their home.

As the call started, tears flowed from students in each of the connected locations around the globe. It's difficult to describe the intensity of the emotions at that moment, but the impact was obvious. For my students, and the others who had worked to obtain the filters for their friends, they had learned the power of using education to help others. Their faces at that moment told me that, for the rest of their lives, they would seek out ways to use learning to make the world a better place.

The Role of Teachers

If we are to achieve the vision of an education system that balances the need for technological relevance with the need for kindness and emotional intelligence, teachers will be paramount. According to Educational Leadership, "During the school year, children generally spend more time interacting with their teachers than with their parents. What happens inside schools has a deep and lasting effect on the mindsets that children develop toward lifelong learning."[19]

Research tells us that teacher effectiveness is the largest in-school factor in student success.[20] At the same time, teachers are constantly influencing the character development of their students both in their capacity as role models and in the interactions they have in their schools.[21] With their vast locus of influence on students in both the academic realm and the area of emotional intelligence, teachers will be the keystone of healthy educational systems.

19 Wolk, Steven (2008). Joy in School. Retrieved November 5, 2017, from www.ascd.org/publications/educational-leadership/sept08/vol66/num01/Joy-in-School.aspx

20 *Teachers Matter: Understanding Teachers' Impact on Student Achievement.* (2012). Santa Monica, CA: RAND Corporation. Retrieved from www.rand.org/pubs/corporate_pubs/CP693z1-2012-09.html

21 Weissbourd, Rick (2003). Moral Teachers, Moral Students. Retrieved November 5, 2017, from www.ascd.org/publications/educational-leadership/mar03/vol60/num06/Moral-Teachers,-Moral-Students.aspx

Data from the OECD Teaching and Learning International Survey (TALIS) study shows that technology has many benefits. It can amplify innovative teaching by expanding access to content, support new pedagogical models, allow wider collaboration for knowledge creation and make feedback faster and more granular.[22] Yet, increased computer usage in schools correlates with lower reading scores.[23] In his plenary address to the Global Education and Skills Form in 2016, Andreas Schleicher, Director for the Directorate of Education and Skills at OECD, explained that technology often does more harm than good in schools today because it hasn't been integrated properly.[24] Clearly, focusing on elevating teaching is more important than increasing technology usage in schools.

Some have suggested that AI is destined to replace teachers in the near future.[25] This is based upon a gross misunderstanding of learning and a fundamental ignorance of the aspects of education that are most important for students to be successful in their lives. The parts of teaching that are most easily automated are also the least important. Our success in education will be measured by the intrinsicity with which our students use learning for good after graduation, a skill that can only be developed in the presence of positive emotional relationships.

Studies that have taken into account the complexities of the teaching profession and its basis in human relationships have determined that robots are very unlikely to possess the ability to do the job well. According to a 2013 Oxford University study,[26] almost half of jobs are in danger of disappearing due to automation, but teaching is among

22 The OECD Teaching and Learning International Survey (TALIS) 2013 Results – Excel Figures and Tables. (n.d.). Retrieved November 5, 2017, from www.oecd.org/edu/school/talis-excel-figures-and-tables.htm
23 Students, Computers and Learning: Making the Connection – en. (n.d.). Retrieved November 5, 2017, from www.oecd.org/publications/students-computers-and-learning-9789264239555-en.htm
24 Schleicher, A. (2016, March 18). Making Education Everybody's Business. Speech presented at Global Education and Skills Forum in United Arab Emirates, Dubai.
25 Radowitz, J. V. (2017, September 11). Intelligent Machines Will Replace Teachers within 10 Years, Leading Public School Headteacher Predicts. Retrieved November 5, 2017, from www.independent.co.uk/news/education/education-news/intelligent-machines-replace-teachers-classroom-10-years-ai-robots-sir-anthony-sheldon-wellington-a7939931.html
26 Frey, C. B. & Osborne, M. A. (2017). The Future of Employment: How Susceptible Are Jobs to Computerisation? *Technological Forecasting and Social Change*, 114: 254–80. doi: 10.1016/j.techfore.2016.08.019.

the professions that is least threatened. The amount of creativity and social intelligence required to teach well is simply too "human" to be done by a machine.

The most important things that teachers do cannot be quantified or digitized easily. Teachers inspire their students to be intrinsically motivated learners, to overcome obstacles in their lives, and to dream big. Teachers see the value in each child that enters their care and the potential that each has to bring joy to others. Teachers recognize the struggles that youngsters have outside school and help them develop the capacity to rise above adversity.

Simply put, teachers love.

It is Stephen Ritz's love of his students that drives him to help them grow their own healthy food in the South Bronx. It is Bijal Damani's love of her students that drives her to help them see the importance of service. It is Emmily Minayo's love of her students that drives her to overcome the difficulties of providing Internet access in the Kibera slum so that her students can experience the world and share their culture with others. It is my love of my students that drives me to keep learning so that I can provide them with the best educational experiences I can.

Computers cannot love. While the health of businesses may depend on the ability to use technology to do tasks faster and more efficiently, our societal health does not. Our global society will depend on how well we recruit, develop and retain excellent teachers, and we are currently in a crisis.

Seventy-four countries currently face an acute teacher shortage, and by 2030, 33 countries will not have enough teachers to provide quality education to all children.[27] In many of our poorest countries, 25 per cent of teachers are untrained.[28] The United Nations estimates that 69 million teachers will need to be recruited and trained in order to meet the Sustainable Development Goal of global universal primary and secondary education.[29] Ensuring the quality of the teachers we

---

27 Teachers Task Force for Education 2030. (n.d.). Retrieved November 5, 2017, from www.teachersforefa.unesco.org/v2/index.php/en/newss/item/490-global-teacher-shortage-threatens-education-2030

28 Coughlan, S. (2014, October 6). Acute Global Teacher Shortage, Warns UN. Retrieved November 5, 2017, from www.bbc.com/news/education-29505581

29 Hodal, K. (2016, October 5). UN Warns Universal Education Goal Will Fail without 69 Million New Teachers. Retrieved November 5, 2017, from www.theguardian.com/global-development/2016/oct/05/un-universal-education-goal-fail-69-million-new-teachers-unesco

recruit to fill this gap will be critical. We must find ways to convince the best talent in each country to teach.

Teachers must be respected in order for education systems to thrive. The TALIS study found that teacher professionalism, including autonomy, content knowledge and opportunity for peer networking, is an indicator of better teacher outcomes in a system. More autonomy is also associated with higher teacher job satisfaction and retention.[30]

When teachers are able to do what they believe is best for students, are compensated in a manner that matches the training and degrees they hold, and have opportunities to use available technology to help students and collaborate with other professional educators around the world, students benefit.

If we focus on elevating the teaching profession, promoting best practices, utilizing technology to inspire students and keeping education rooted in the best of our humanity, I am optimistic that we will look back at this time in history as a positive turning point in the creation of a harmonious and prosperous global society.

As Elisa will show us in the next chapter, technology is an important tool, but it is the human or emotional element that only teachers can bring that ensures a successful education. If we get that aspect of education right, all of our children will be well.

30 Sparks, D. & Malkus, N. (2015). Public School Teacher Autonomy in the Classroom across School Years 2003–04, 2007–08, and 2011–12 (Rep. No. NCES 2015089). Washington, DC: National Center for Education Statistics.

Chapter 2

Education Today

A Collection of Snapshots

Elisa Guerra

It's been less than 36 hours since a major earthquake hit southern and central México. The airport in México City shows some cracks and tears here and there, but is already in operation. Some areas have been isolated with yellow tape alerting people to stay away. A few glass windows and doors are shattered, testifying for the magnitude of the tremor.

I'm sitting near my boarding gate. There is a TV blasting on, live from a fallen school in which attempts are being made to rescue children from the rubble. As a mother, a teacher and a Mexican, my heart hurts deeply. I also feel vulnerable and restless. The look in other passengers' faces tells me I'm not the only one.

The earth has, quite literally, shattered below our feet. Along with the sense of loss and mourning comes the opportunity to heal and mend what has been broken. I can't help but think of the countless things that have gone through upheaval lately, both literally and metaphorically. How many of them remain broken and dysfunctional? Could education be one of them?

A few hours later, I am standing in front of an immigration officer in Toronto. It is early morning, and after a sleepless red-eye flight, I know that the face the officer is staring at is not my best. "What brings you to Canada?" he asks as he carefully inspects my Mexican passport. I tell him I am scheduled to speak at a conference with other international teachers about inequity in education. He demands to see the conference invitation, my hotel reservation and my ticket to go back home. He asks some more questions and finally lets me go.

What I did not tell him is that I will also be meeting with those same teaching colleagues from around the world to work on a book we are writing and that I am charged with writing a chapter describing school education as it is today in relation to the Fourth Industrial Revolution – a monumental task.

Lucy's Frog

If we want to define or at least sketch a path for schools to arrive into 2030, we need to have an idea of where we are right now. It is a globalized world we are living, but the experience of school is perceived very differently depending on which part of the planet you are located. It would be naïve to try to explain global education today from my limited view as a teacher in Aguascalientes, the belly button of Mexico. To put in as many voices as possible I consulted research documents and designed a survey to be answered by the finalists of the Global Teacher Prize, from 2015 to 2017.

I also interviewed experts in the field. Professor Eduardo Andere has probably seen more classrooms than anyone else in the world. He has been in the guts of more than 300 schools in 26 countries, observing and interviewing teachers, principals and education experts. The results of his extensive research have been published in books and papers. Lucy Crehan is a British educator and international consultant who has taught in five PISA (Programme for International Student Assessment) top-performing education systems, later sharing experiences and insights in her book *Cleverlands*. Gabriela Kaplan is the coordinator for the English learning program at Ceibal, a government initiative using technology to remotely teach thousands of students in Uruguay. These three experts shared their ideas and views on the reality of education from their unique perspectives. Their words will accompany us through most of this chapter. In *Cleverlands*, Lucy Crehan (2016)[1] writes about the Chinese story of a frog that lived at the bottom of a well. One day, a bird came by to the side of the well and asked the frog, "What do you see?"

The frog answered: "I see the sky. It is so small."

Bird was dismayed. "Oh, no! The sky is very big!"

Crehan then goes on to compare the common "Western perception of Chinese education" to the perception of the frog: while able to see the sky, only a tiny view of it is in his knowledge. How inaccurate it is to judge a whole by a minuscule bit. This is precisely the risk of presenting a single picture of education today – therefore, I will aim to showcase instead a collection of snapshots, however blurry, of where are schools positioned at the threshold of the Fourth Industrial Revolution.

---

1 Crehan, L. (2016). *Cleverlands: The Secrets behind the Success of the World's Education Superpowers*. London: Unbound.

There is a coffee shop around the corner from the Library at NYU, in Manhattan. I am sipping a latte, while my interviewee, Doctor Eduardo Andere, holds a green tea frappe. It's late summer, and in many places around the world schools, are about to start. There is a comfortable afternoon breeze.

After receiving graduate degrees from Harvard and Boston College, Dr. Andere transitioned from focusing in law, economics, public administration and political science into education. He served as Deputy Director General for International Affairs at Mexico's National Science and Technology Foundation (CONACYT) and as Executive Director for the US–Mexico Fulbright Program. Currently a visiting scholar at the Steinhart School of Culture, Education and Human Development at New York University, he has published 12 books on comparative education and education policy.

Successful School Systems

Almost all the education systems Dr. Andere has visited are among the highest ranking on international tests,[2] with a few exceptions, including his native Mexico and Chile. I am curious to learn if he has identified some common traits for success.

"There is no silver bullet," he says.

I found successful schools on both opposite sides of the pedagogical spectrum: progressive and traditional. But there are two problems with success: The first one is related to its definition. The more we define success with easy-to-measure outcomes, i.e., standardized tests, the less insightful the measure is. The more thorough we define success the more difficult to measure, no matter how sophisticated the measures are from the statistical point of view. Teachers and principals in general lean on thorough rather than narrow measures. Teachers and principals everywhere see a limitation and a danger to education brought about by standardization. The more policy makers rely on league tables and competition among schools, the more teachers and schools will teach-to-the-test. The most important common trait is the rejection of policies

2 Andere, E. (2008). *The Lending Power of PISA: League Tables and Best Practice in International Education.* CERC Monograph Series in Comparative and International Education and Development. No. 6. Hong Kong, China: The University of Hong Kong.

that put pressure on schools and teachers based on the globalization argument. Teachers and principals think that standardized-oriented policy makers miss the main or core pedagogical point of school education.

Therefore, to answer the question "What do successful schools have in common?" Dr. Andere adds:

> We need to answer first what we mean by success. If success is measured by standardized tests followed by accountability policies such as rewards or punishments or even domestic or international league tables, successful schools look like the Singaporean or Korean schools: A lot of competitive pressure on students, teachers and schools to perform high, very high. Teachers and students are specifically driven and trained to test-oriented education systems. And indeed, they perform very high in these types of contests or competitions such as PISA, TIMSS and PIRLS. If success is measured by a combination of factors, including tests, but also projects, progress, effort, attitudes and competencies, the narrative about the students' and schools' performance is the best way to measure schools. Here schools, teachers and students are much more concentrated on the learning and teaching process than on the outcomes. Teachers are more focused on children's growth than on their performance in tests.

The question about what high-performing schools have in common is also the first I ask Lucy Crehan. We held the interview on Skype; it's morning for me, early afternoon for her in the United Kingdom. Her book on vivid anecdotes about teaching in Japan, China, Singapore, Finland and Canada, intertwined with research and data, is a fascinating read. Crehan politely rephrases my question, with just a little tweak: instead of "high-performing schools," she prefers to talk about "high-performing systems." She tells me she has identified at least five shared traits:

- All the systems she visited start formal education at 6 or 7, and most offer high-quality preschool programs – a solid base before formal education.
- Particularly the high-performing nations in Asia have a mastery-based curriculum, which means that they go into quite a lot of depth as opposed to breadth, especially in the first few years of schooling.

- They have high expectations for all students. "It sounds clichéd," Crehan says, "but there is a difference between high hopes and high expectations." She goes on to explain that with the exception of Singapore, these systems are not tracking students into different schools or even different classes until age 15 or 16. In other words, they are setting quite high standards that they expect all children to achieve all the way up to the end of compulsory education. Of course, high expectations, by themselves, won't get all kids to achieve, but there are other policies in place to make that happen. For example, having qualified teachers – instead of teaching assistants – to support students that are struggling.
- These systems treat teachers as professionals. There are high standards on entry to the profession, and extensive pre-service training. Teachers are assessed both on subject knowledge and practical skills. Then, it is easier to give teachers autonomy, because you know what they have been through to get there.
- Accountability measures are used for growth and improvement rather than punishment and reward. Whether a school is performing well or is struggling, the response is not prizes or sanctions, but strategies to help the school thrive and improve.

A Decade of Change?

Time allows for greater perspective. A longitudinal study that focused on education systems in 2004 and then recaptured data again a decade later has shown Dr. Andere the incredible changes that have occurred in the early part of this century.

"Schools and teachers are definitely more inclined to a thorough view of education rather than a standardized view of education," he states. "There is much more concentration on human interactions, the human learning environment and the emotional part of education than on performance on domestic or international tests." There is also a growing concern about the pre-service training of teachers and how high school students can be attracted to become educators. We can almost hear a universal outcry to dignify the teaching profession.

After ten years of visiting the same or similar schools, I was able to see some changes in the learning environments: There are more information and communication technology (ICT) devices in schools, although they are still figuring out the best way to use them. New schools have become much more imaginative about the physical learning environments (more open and polyvalent spaces; more time and space for collaborative work). Principals and local educational authorities encourage teachers to establish professional learning communities. There is also much more collaboration among teachers not only in planning but also in teaching and learning. And, of course, there is also an unstoppable drive to make teaching a professional activity, such as physicians, lawyers, scientists or engineers. The more teachers are attracted, trained and certified as professionals, the less the need for accountability measures. This means that teachers and principals will be pedagogically empowered.

Dr. Andere's findings suggest that students are much more active in planning and learning activities. Schools and teachers are more concerned about global and multicultural issues, and there is a widespread understanding that "education is not enough."[3] Schools and teachers are more aware and critical about their own work. Schools, teachers and students are trying to make schools less monotonous.

Two important aspects of education systems have remained constant, Dr. Andere continues:

> First, teachers are much more important than technology. According to most teachers' and principals' perspectives, "personalized technological assisted learning" is a myth. Schools and teachers are not saying "no" to technology: they are merely limiting its power as a function of pedagogy). Some teachers and experts even call this "depersonalized learning" to stress the fact that human interaction is crucial for learning.

Second, the more motivated students are, the less elaborate physical and technological learning environments need to be in schools. Motivated students will do the work and put the necessary effort to succeed, regardless of how success is defined.

Could motivation be a greater factor than technology in influencing student performance? It seems intuitive that this is the case. Research

---

3 Attributed to Levin and Kelley and cited by Andere, E. (2008). *The Lending Power of PISA: League Tables and Best Practice in International Education.* CERC Monograph Series in Comparative and International Education and Development. No. 6. Hong Kong, China: The University of Hong Kong, p. 30.

has shown that investment in ICT use in schools correlates with limited, and sometimes negative, "traditional performance indicators, such as test scores, grades in national examinations, and incidence of dropout."[4]

Crehan says her experiences support this statement. "I did not see a substantial use of ICT in any of the systems I visited, with the exception of Canada." But even there, the use of technology was rather scarce, and mostly as a result of teachers' own drive, and not a systemic schoolwide use.

Will this change anytime soon? Will teachers and schools succumb or rise in the Fourth Industrial Revolution? Dr. Andere offers some reflections:

What has been dubbed as the 4IR – more digitalization, more sophistication, more interconnectedness among different technologies, more opportunities for productivity and communication – will surely become part of the schools of tomorrow. Not today. Schools are still trying to understand what to do with the level of digitalization brought about by the Third Industrial Revolution. However, schools and education policy makers are beginning to realize that digitization (software and hardware) has to be included as a new language in school curricula. Policy makers are beginning to ask the following question: Do we want our regular students to be savvy about the use of digital devices – mainly as consumers – or do we want them to learn the digitalization language so they can improve and innovate the digitization devices and processes – as creators? Other than that, almost all teachers and principals told me that we'll have to wait at least another 10 to 20 years to see new shifts in technology use in schools.

It seems that whenever there is a trend, schools tend to be the last to embrace it – if ever. This can be both good and bad. Of course, we would not want our education systems to jump into novelty for novelty's sake. Schools usually lean on the conservative side: change is many times more difficult and slower than it can be in other organizations – and it is already hard to embrace it everywhere. Instead of playing catch-up all the time, we need to keep up with technology as it races ahead. But in too many cases, schools' computer labs look more like warehouses for discontinued models.

4 OECD. (2015). *Students, Computers and Learning: Making the Connection*, PISA, OECD Publishing. http://dx.doi.org/10.1787/9789264239555-en

On Teachers and Technology

Some time ago, I was invited to write an article for WISE EdReview. The topic was fascinating but not new: Could technology ever replace teachers?[5] After all, it is already impacting many other professions out there.

Would you rather have a great teacher or great technology for learning? Many would argue that technology has reduced the need for teachers. After all, most of the world's cumulative knowledge is now just a click away.

But, can you find it? And once you do, can you recognize the valuable and true among the irrelevant in disguise? Can our children and youngsters take charge of their own education? And even more important: Are teachers responsible for just the transmission of knowledge, which can now be so "easily" accessed?

If you need to learn a new skill or gain solid knowledge about something, having a caring mentor beside you can make all the difference. Having both the teacher and the technology might further advance learning. But not necessarily, according to Organisation for Economic Cooperation and Development (OECD).[6] Their research has shown that there were no significant improvements in students' academic achievement in the countries with heavy investments in ICT for education. This tells us that owning the hardware and software is not enough.

Technology has great potential for improving education. It can easily connect people from across the globe and allow learners to witness the world in a way not possible before. It can provide education opportunities to those far away. And certainly, it has greatly contributed to the expansion of knowledge. But could technology eventually take the place of teachers?

It is not likely. In his foreword for the above-mentioned 2015 OECD report, Andreas Schleicher states that "technology can amplify great teaching, but technology cannot replace poor teaching." Good teaching, because it is based on building relationships, is even less likely to be replicated by computer programs.

Teachers, like all other professionals, have always relied on an array of tools to do their job. They look for any opportunity to better serve their students. Books, pencils, paper and chalkboards are traditional

5 Guerra, E. (2016). Can Great Technologies Replace Great Teaching? *WISE EdReview*. Retrieved October 31, 2017, from www.wise-qatar.org/can-great-technologies-replace-great-teaching-elisa-guerra

6 OECD. (2015). *Students, Computers and Learning: Making the Connection*, PISA, OECD Publishing. http://dx.doi.org/10.1787/9789264239555-en

examples of tools that were at one time considered "new technology." But technology, however developed, is still a tool. Or, as Dunn and Dunn eloquently say, "The technology is not the lesson, it is there to enhance the lesson."[7] In other words, technology is not the teacher. It is there to assist the teacher.

Insisting that technology will replace teachers is like saying that the hammer will replace the carpenter. Yes, a machine could produce a piece of furniture in a standardized way much faster than a single carpenter could. But children are not pieces of furniture, mass-produced to a standard. Children need the artistic touch of human connection to reach their unique potential. And that comes from either a teacher, a parent, or both.

Dr. Andere asked teachers and principals whether they thought technology would eventually replace teachers.[8] The overwhelming answer was no. Is that just wishful thinking, or do educators really have a point?

The reality of implementing excellent classroom technology does not fit the romantic vision of kids dreamily displaying interactive apps on shiny new tablets and lessons flowing smoothly with little effort from the teacher. In fact, integrating technology to one's classroom is exceedingly difficult, requiring ongoing learning, creativity and a risk-taking mentality. There must also be ample access to Internet and devices. Most teachers already using technology in their schools realize that they are working more, not less. Furthermore, "technology can only do so much. It can be transient and can become obsolete very quickly. What is a constant, though, is the teacher in the classroom."[9]

Even great technology will not replace teachers, good or bad. But it will certainly, over time, change the way we teach. It has already revolutionized the way we work and live. And, although computers will not replace teachers, "teachers who do not use technology will be replaced by those who do."[10]

Technology will offer teachers an overwhelming whirlwind of opportunities and challenges, while also demanding educators grow as professionals to adapt to new trends. Will technology deliver its promise of better outcomes in education for everyone? Given access and proper training, the answer then lies within the teachers.

---

7 Dunn, J. & Dunn, K. (2013). Technology Will Not Replace Teachers. *Huffpost Impact.*
8 Andere, E. (2016). *¿Cómo es el aprendizaje en escuelas de clase mundial?* [How Is Learning in World-Class Schools?] Volume I & II. México: Pearson.
9 Wright, P. (2013). Why New Technologies Could Never Replace Great Teaching.
10 Trucano, M. (2015). Will Technology Replace Teachers? No, but . . . World Bank. Edutech.

Teaching in the Time of Internet

To see how technology can be used beneficially, I met Gabriela Kaplan at the Bett Latin American Summit in México City, after she had delivered a lecture titled "Schools in action: Using technology for ESL learning." We had a lively conversation at dinner that night as I interviewed her over salad and salmon. I was impressed by the remarks in her lecture. Ceibal, a government funded initiative, currently helps more than one hundred thousand students from grade through high school learn English remotely. Although the subject teacher is on the other side of a screen, there is always an educator present in the room at all times. Each class has their own "virtual" English teacher, who stays with them for every lesson throughout the year. Lessons are conducted in real time, which makes it easier to interact and bond. The teacher can also see the students on screen, and even zoom in to a particular child if needed. During the lecture, Kaplan showed a photo where eye-to-eye contact was being made between the two teachers, with students in the background. "Collaboration is key," she stressed. Ceibal is not replacing the teacher with technology. It is using technology to take the teacher to the students.

It seems to be working – not only for driving learning, but also for reducing inequity. In Kaplan's own words:

> Technology is a great tool that may help provide more equity for our students. It cannot however do it on its own, it requires humans who are honestly seeking equity to achieve so. In our program, we have seen children from very complex socio-cultural surroundings gain knowledge, even at a faster pace than children in other contexts, albeit between the second and third year in the program, and never quite reaching the same levels.

This means that while technology is helping to close the achievement gap, by itself is not enough. Complete data can be found in Ceibal's English Adaptive Assessment (2016).[11]

Teachers' Voices

Both Dr. Andere and Ms. Crehan have predominantly visited schools in high-achieving education systems. But there is still much more of the sky for the frog to see. What about the countries that do not make

---

11 Ceibal. (2016). English Adaptive Assessment, Executive Summary. Retrieved October 31, 2017, from http://ingles.ceibal.edu.uy/wp-content/uploads/2017/04/2016-English-Adaptive.pdf

PISA's honour roll? What about the ones that are not even tested? And how do insiders perceive their own school experiences as educators wherever in the world they are located?

To get a broader view of the impact of technology on learning in diverse environments around the world, our team asked former Global Teacher Prize finalists to complete a survey. Responses came from 42 teachers in 25 different countries. The countries represented were Afghanistan, Argentina, Belgium, Brazil, Canada, Chile, Colombia, Estonia, India, Italy, Japan, Kenya, Latvia, Macedonia, Malaysia, Mexico, Paraguay, Peru, Philippines, Poland, Romania, Sierra Leone, Spain, United Kingdom and United States.

Although we could not consider the respondents to represent the average teacher in their countries – as they were selected into the group precisely for being outstanding – their narratives in many cases include not only their own experiences, but also their perceptions on the realities of their schools and systems.

The teachers answering our survey have an average of 19.26 years as educators, a total of 809 human years of cumulative experience. The longest teaching career in the group is 32 years, the shortest, 4 years. Their average age is 43, with a range of 28 to 61.

Most of these teachers work in urban schools (60%). Two-thirds (66%) work in public schools. More than half work in secondary and high schools, while a third teaches in elementary schools. A smaller percentage of them are early childhood educators or college professors. Sixteen per cent of the teachers also hold administrative and leadership positions.

Close to half (45%) of the teachers work with children from low to very low socioeconomic backgrounds. Thirty-eight per cent of them teach students from middle to middle-high classes. Ten per cent work with special needs, refugee or hospitalized children. Only 7 per cent teach privileged youths, coming from high socioeconomic backgrounds.

Sixty nine per cent of the respondents' schools provide Internet access for everyone, students included. Twenty-one per cent allows only teachers and staff to connect, and 10 per cent have no Internet access at all.

We asked educators how big was the role of technology both at their schools and in their own teaching. Sixty per cent of respondents said that technology plays a role of 75 per cent to 100 per cent of their teaching activities, but when asked about their perception of how much was technology being used schoolwide, only 35 per cent declared its role in the same range of 75 per cent to 100 per cent. This shows that, for our respondents, technology plays a bigger role in their teaching than it does for the average educator within their schools. It also tells us that, ultimately and for this sample, it is the teacher who decides how much and how to use technology in the classroom, and that ICT's use is not a main part of the school's culture – yet.

Figures 2.1 and 2.2 show the answers to this question:

How big is the role of technology in your own teaching/schoolwide? (The more you use technology every day and for a wide array of activities both with and without your students, in school context, the larger role it plays.) Please provide an estimate of the percentage your/school work relies on ICT:

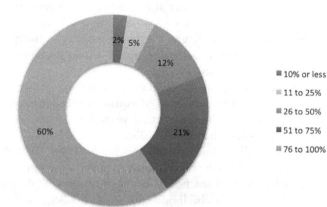

Figure 2.1 Role of technology in own teaching

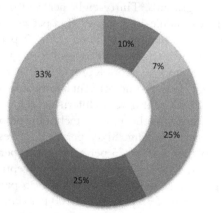

Figure 2.2 Role of technology, schoolwide

Among the respondents, the use of technology for their professional activities is on the rise − 74 per cent of them reported that they use ICT "a lot more" than 15 years ago. The same number of teachers expect their use to keep rising expansively.

However, teachers did not see technology replacing them anytime soon. Consistent with Dr. Andere's findings, the vast majority of our teachers (93%) responded no to the question: "Do you think that technology will eventually replace teachers?" Two teachers replied yes; however, they stressed that technology would replace only "part" of the teacher's job − or that the educator's role would be redefined. Dana Narvaiša, from Latvia, wrote: "Instead of teachers, we will need mentors, supervisors that help students acquire learning and social skills − but not knowledge."

The tasks that could be somewhat easily assigned to Artificial Intelligence (AI) are mostly administrative − grading papers, tracking attendance, data collection − and even classroom cleaning, says Michael Wamaya, from Kenya. But, he adds, AI could never develop an "emotional attachment to students" − which all respondents recognize as paramount for successful teaching. Glenn Wagner, from Canada, writes:

> Understanding how to form positive teacher–student relationships has shown a very high effect in classroom learning. Reciprocal teaching, the act of teaching each other basically, is another research-tested powerful practice. . . . Notice that these major strategies are all about human–human relationships. Technology may help to facilitate but it is all about the interactions that take place between people.

How technology is used in each classroom varies wildly. Joe Fatheree, from the United States, writes:

> We have a technology-enriched classroom. I have my own private lab. My students utilize every form of recording software to create short films and produce original music. We have access to 3D printers, CNC machines, drones, Minecraft, and a myriad of other tools. However, I want to point out that technology is just that − a series of tools. The focus of the class is to help our students to discover their potential. Technology is quite frankly only a small part of that experience. The other work we do is much more important as it is how we create a climate that helps students believe they can do the

impossible. It is that type of mindset that will lead to the cure for cancer, end global warming, and solve a host of other issues.

On the other side of the spectrum, Azizullah Royesh, from Afghanistan, reports the role of technology in his classrooms as "very little, near to nothing." Miriam Mason, from Sierra Leone, writes: "We pre-prepare learning materials using computers but apart from that technology does not often enter the classroom. Maybe we will use phones for videoing or photos to be shared with donors, partners or as part of a project, but the students nor teachers are using technology more than that." And Jacqueline Jumbe-Kahura, from Kenya, adds: "I do not use technology because we have neither the technology nor electricity at school. But I use technology to enhance my teaching and explore varied ways of teaching and learning." It is humbling to note that even in environments devoid of technology, excellent pedagogy is still leading to astonishing student learning outcomes.

But, on the whole, technology plays a large role in the classroom. Most of the teachers used ICT and devices such as tablets, laptops, cameras, projectors, smart boards and printers. Many have created, along with their students, a vast array of products such as eBooks, videos, websites and digital startups. Some teachers have "flipped" the classroom, combining live and digital lessons. A few, like David Calle, from Spain, teach almost exclusively online.

"In my observations and interviews I found that technology is growing more rapidly than the pedagogical ability of teachers to use it," stresses Dr. Andere. He continues:

> Schools and teachers are using more technological devices and software than ever before. However, there is not yet a paradigm about the best way to use ITC in schools. Even within the same educational system or district there is a huge variety of technological uses. Given this fact, policy makers are beginning to realize that the best public policy decision is not to invest in ITC gadgets but on ITC training for teachers. Once teachers are highly trained, let teachers, as professionals, decide about the best way to choose and use information and communication technologies.

The Best and Worst

When asked to describe best and worst practices in education today, we find a consensus on the dark side. Steve Remington, from Canada, refers to "static learning," where students have limited interaction with their peers and community to apply skills, as opposed to "engaged learning." There is also an outcry against "excessive testing" and too much "curriculum-oriented instruction." Nathan Atkinson, from England, sums it up: "The worst practices are one-size-fits-all teaching and teaching to the test."

As for best practices, empowering students, using a wide inventory of strategies and building strong relationships with the students were recognized as key.

When asked about best and worst practices in education now, Dr. Andere's responses were in line with those of the world teachers. For best practices, he describes schools that are

> more active, more collaborative, more concerned about the bal ance of cognitive and non-cognitive learning; more concentrated on teachers' quality than teachers' performance; more conscious about the limits of education and the need for a more comprehensive view of education, i.e. school, home and community learning environments. There is also a widespread concern about multiculturalism and the fact of globalization. Globalization is a phenomenon and a fact; it is not an opinionated view of the world.

Frenetic use of standardized testing and accountability based on tests and league tables were mentioned as the system's worst practices. Dr. Andere also warns that

> there is one exogenous menace to schools and education: the view from the outside world that the pedagogical variables respond more or less to the same principles as the business and economic variables. Outsiders to the pedagogical world think that children's brains react the same way as adults' brains. Adults compete; adults live in a zero-sum game when they make economic or business transactions; they operate in the extrinsic motivation world. Children will become adults; but that doesn't mean that they should be trained to behave as adults while they are growing up. So, the worst practice today is to treat schools as factories or business, and children as adults.

What, then, should students learn to be better equipped for the challenges of our times and for the future? A whole new world opens. Teachers' responses were as enthusiastic as they were diverse: global citizenship, soft skills, environmental awareness, digital literacy, critical thinking, relationships, teamwork, entrepreneurship and even meditation!

Are We There Yet?

So, we think we know what students should learn and how we should teach them. Are we there yet? Is that the reality of our schools around the world? Of course, it is not – and it might never fully be. Many challenges threaten the very core of education. Irrelevant curricula, mechanized methodologies and standardized testing excesses play a part, and so do poverty, inequity and political extremism. But, as Michael will demonstrate in the next chapter, there is a greater danger; in a divided world where 17 per cent of people live without electricity, arguments about the use of technology can seem irrelevant to those left behind. However, as he will describe, true educational success lies in a system that meets the needs of the individual, with or without the use of technology.

The technological march is unstoppable. Wherever each school is placed, and however willing or unwilling, we are all somehow at the edge of monumental change. There is no way back.

Then, what shall we do when we are standing at the precipice?

We dare to fly.

Chapter 3

Overcoming Equity Gaps in and through Education

Michael Soskil

In the Namasoko Primary School on the outskirts of a village in Southern Malawi, Andrews Nchessie's students weren't coming to school. The
children were forced by a devastating famine to spend their days scroung-
ing the scorched plains for food. Attending school had become a luxury
that they could not afford. In his country where 90 per cent of people
live on less than US$ 2 per day, and there are over 46,000 malnourished
children, Andrews was frustrated that his students were starving. Starving
for food to eat. Starving for a life where they could enjoy childhood.
Starving for the opportunity to get an education that would be their only
chance to escape the hopelessness they were feeling. For those students,
their basic survival was in doubt. Using tools of the Fourth Industrial
Revolution to prepare them for a rapidly changing global workforce was
the last thing on the minds of their teachers, parents or community.

Ever widening inequity will be one of the gravest threats to the
health of our future society, and one of the most difficult problems
to overcome within our current economic, education and social systems. Even now, while those in affluent societies struggle to keep up
with exploding technological advances, 17 per cent of the planet still
lives without electricity. Global income disparity is at an all-time high,
with the 62 wealthiest individuals controlling more than the bottom
50 per cent of the world's population.[1] This growing divide between
those who benefit from rapid technological innovation and those

1 Hardoon, D., Fuentes-Nieva, R. & Ayele, S. (2016, January 18). An Economy for the
1%: How Privilege and Power in the Economy Drive Extreme Inequality and How This
Can Be Stopped. Oxfam, GB. Retrieved November 5, 2017, from http://policy-practice.
oxfam.org.uk/publications/an-economy-for-the-1-how-privilege-and-power-in-the-
economy-drive-extreme-inequ-592643

who fall further behind threatens the health of our increasingly global society. Richard Wilkinson, in his book *The Spirit Level*, shows that high inequality correlates with high crime rates, distrust of others, lack of opportunity and mental illness.[2] These problems will pass to our children, and we must provide them not just with technological proficiency and critical thinking skills, but also with compassion for their fellow man. Klaus Schwab concludes: "In the end it comes down to people, culture, and values. Indeed, we need to work very hard to ensure that all citizens across cultures, nations and income groups understand the need to master the fourth industrial revolution and its civilizational challenges."[3]

Both the United Nations Educational, Scientific and Cultural Organization (UNESCO) and the World Economic Forum (WEF) have stressed the importance of equity for a prosperous future. In the WEF's Incheon Declaration of 2015, inclusion and equity were listed as "the cornerstone of a transformative education agenda."[4] The UN's Sustainable Development Goal 4 seeks to "ensure inclusive and equitable quality education and promote lifelong learning opportunities for all" by 2030.[5] Yet, during the Fourth Industrial Revolution, inequity in society and education is expanding at the rate of innovation. "Competition" and "cooperation" are antonyms, and our current systems are built upon the former. If we are to realize the peaceful and prosperous vision of our future we desire, a focus on equity through and within our educational systems must be one of our main driving forces.

Education is both the problem and the solution. Disadvantaged populations who are denied equal access to quality education become increasingly marginalized as technology innovation leads to higher-education requirements for jobs that pay a living wage. However, when we use education as a tool to close the divisive gaps in our society conditions are created in which an individual's effort, rather than his or her background, determines success. Augusto Lopez-Claros, director of the Global Indicators Group at the World Bank Group, explains:

2 Wilkinson, R. & Pickett, K. (n.d.). The Spirit Level: Why Greater Equality Makes Societies Stronger Kindle Edition. Retrieved November 5, 2017, from www.amazon.com/dp/B003TWOK70/ref=dp-kindle-redirect?_encoding=UTF8&btkr=1
3 Schwab, K. (2017). *The Fourth Industrial Revolution*. New York: Crown Business.
4 Incheon Declaration. (2015). Retrieved November 5, 2017, from http://en.unesco.org/world-education-forum-2015/incheon-declaration
5 UNESCO and Sustainable Development Goals. (2017, June 27). Retrieved November 5, 2017, from http://en.unesco.org/sdgs

The most sustainable path towards ending extreme poverty and promoting shared prosperity is through creating an inclusive society, allowing everyone, including traditionally marginalized groups such as ethnic, religious, and other minorities, the same opportunity to participate in and benefit from the economy.[6]

Equality of opportunity is our path to prosperity in the Fourth Industrial Revolution.

The Challenges of Data-Driven Decision Making

Right now, data driven by technological growth are fueling economic expansion in the Fourth Industrial Revolution. The greater the speed of innovation, the greater the gap becomes between those who are benefitting and those who are left behind. In an environment fueled by competition and accumulating wealth, this works exceedingly well. However, when the goal is to provide opportunity to the widest number of people possible, and to help individuals overcome disadvantages, this presents complicated issues that must be addressed.

Inés Bulacio sees this challenge every day in her work with hospitalized children in Argentina. Her students cannot attend schools due to their conditions, but the nurture she has provided them combined with imaginative uses for technology have led to powerful outcomes. Her students learn through project-based lessons in which they use technology tools and social media to create videos and share their stories with others. Their work informs the medical professionals who are treating similar illnesses in other children, helps their parents understand how they are internally handling the struggle of dealing with their condition and allows them to share their situation with classmates at the schools they cannot attend. Required curriculum is intentionally infused into those projects to ensure that each student progresses.

According to Carina Omoeva of the Education Equity Research Initiative, disabled children like Inés's students are among the groups least represented in available datasets used to close equity gaps, and the data that are available have consistency issues that make it difficult

6 Lopez-Claros, A. (2015, July 29). Equality of Opportunity as an Engine of Prosperity. Retrieved November 5, 2017, from http://blogs.worldbank.org/developmenttalk/equality-opportunity-engine-prosperity

to compare.[7] Finding meaningful conclusions in the limited data that are available is almost impossible due to the many variables that effect the experience of each disabled child. The type of disability, financial situation of the family, emotional makeup of the child, values of the community and thousands of other factors will have an impact on learning. Skilled teachers like Inés, who have personal relationships with students, can understand these variables much better than those looking at the data from afar.

The ability to take risks is as valuable as any form of capital in our current environment. Growth requires innovation, and innovation cannot happen without risk. Economic systems that thrive on competition work well to increase wealth for those fortunate enough to benefit. The strongest companies survive and become models for others to build upon. Companies unable to adapt to current conditions die off leaving space for others. In this type of system, the least affluent individuals, companies and countries are the most risk averse. Without intentional steps to prevent it, a natural side effect of such a system is inequity. Those with capital use it to make more. Those without continue to lack opportunity.

The wealthiest systems, schools and regions are the most able to take risks. They innovate, provide the newest technology to students, and experiment with the newest pedagogical models, constantly improving. The "have-nots" are starved of resources with community school closings in disadvantaged areas. These reforms create winners and losers, just like the business models they are erroneously based upon. However, developing human capital is much more complex than growing financial capital. If our society is to survive and thrive, we must strive for a system where we fight to ensure there are no "losers" in education, and a culture of improvement is provided for every student, teacher and school.

So, how can the use of data help us create a fairer education system? Easily collected quantitative data are necessary to show us where equity gaps are occurring, but they cannot tell us why they are occurring. Only by actually talking with people and analyzing their responses can we effectively work towards a system in which all members of the community have equal opportunity. David Barth, a leading figure in

---

7 Omoeva, C. (2017, September 26). Equity in and through Education: What Are the Issues? Plenary address presented at International Education Funders Group Meeting in University of Toronto, Toronto, Canada.

international development, has spent decades working to strengthen outcomes and opportunities for young people and help them realize their potential to be forces for positive change. Much of that work has included collecting and analyzing data to determine the best utilization of limited resources.

David stresses the need for data to illuminate where our beliefs, stated in constitutions and mission statements, do not match the lived experiences of individuals. At the same time, he warns, "Data is fundamental, but statistics lie." The most valuable datasets, in his opinion, are those democratically defined by those one is looking to serve. Talking with students and teachers to determine the reasons for the equity gaps we see in quantitative datasets is vital if we wish to address the causes of those gaps. David explains: "We cannot get quality qualitative data without input from those in the trenches."[8]

In many places facing significant equity gaps, the status of teachers in society is low.[9] Teachers who are underpaid, undervalued and overworked are less likely to agree to participate in data collection or to innovate solutions. This, in turn, has a negative impact on the quality of data collected, Yet, David's experience has shown him that most teachers are driven to have a positive impact on their students regardless of pay or status. In one example, he shares that a random control trial of new pedagogical models was ruined by compassionate and committed teachers in Liberia. Two adjacent villages were chosen for the experiment. In one, teachers were asked to use an innovative new teaching method. Teachers in the other village were the control group and were expected to continue their normal classroom practices. When the control teachers heard that there were new teaching methods being used in the next village, they snuck over to find out what they were to bring them back. Despite being asked to maintain their current practices for the fidelity of the trial, they believed their students deserved the best teaching practices available. The trial failed to generate useful data, but children benefitted anyway.

If we are to solve the complex issues we face to close equity gaps, data will be necessary to provide context to the nuanced conversations we must have. As the ubiquity of information allows us to insulate our perspective from that which makes us uncomfortable, data

8 Interview with David Barth [Telephone interview]. (2017, October 24).
9 Global Teacher Status Index. (2013). Retrieved November 5, 2017, from www.varkey foundation.org/teacherindex

give us a baseline for discussion. Once that baseline is established, discussion can commence on the meaning and action that must be taken. It is essential that we understand the limitations and biases of the data we use, however. No data are without bias. Many of the most important aspects of education are not quantifiable, and must be protected and elevated despite the fact that they will never appear in a spreadsheet.

Inability to account for bias in data can have devastating consequences. Computers and algorithms, and the data they produce, are often viewed as objective. However, every algorithm that is programmed into a computer is done so by a human bringing their own biases to that process. According to the *Michigan Journal of Race & Law*:

> Computer programs – algorithms coded by humans into a form a computer's chipset can interpret – are written with the objectives, design choices, and general experiences of the programmer as background. The series of instructions, data structures, and design choices that end up in a finished computer program can often translate subtle biases, often in unexpected ways.[10]

Those "unexpected" consequences often widen existing equity gaps, or create new ones. In an environment with limited resources, every data-driven decision we make about where to deploy our resources impacts both the population receiving resources and all of those who are not.

There will always be a fine line between using the data we collect well and using it dangerously. Like in education, humanity and empathy must remain at the heart of our decision making if we are to successfully navigate the challenges of the Fourth Industrial Revolution. Empowering those who are marginalized will mean providing increased democratic control over data production and resource allocation, while increasing transparency over the entire process. Technology is giving consumers the ability to gather unprecedented amounts of data on items before they are purchased. Communities deserve the same access to information about their school systems if they are to be empowered to demand the positive changes that will result in equality of opportunity for all.

---

10 Vagle, J. L. (2016). Tightening the OODA Loop: Police Militarization, Race, and Algorithmic Surveillance. *Michigan. Journal Race & Law*, 22: 101.

Overcoming Traditional Systemic Inequities

While our need to address inequities is paramount to our future success, systemic inequity has long been harming our societal health. When majority populations control systems they tend to impose their identities and values on minority populations. This has been a characteristic of our education systems since their inception. Indigenous populations, minority religious groups, LGBTQ children, immigrants and racial minorities have traditionally suffered due to lack of representation in schools and disadvantages outside of schools that affect in-school performance. Regardless of background, most school-aged children share a desire to acquire an education so that they can successfully compete in the job market and contribute to their community. It is in our best interest as a society to build structures into our educational mission to make this goal attainable for all. In fact, our future depends upon it.

We must strive to ensure that protections for our most vulnerable populations are built into our systems, help those in power understand the importance of equity to all stakeholders and increase minority representation in positions of authority. Each student in our schools deserves teachers in their school who can relate to his or her life. They also need to see leadership positions filled with those from all socioeconomic and minority groups if they are to be empowered to see themselves and each of their peers as having leadership potential. When children have a teacher who comes from the same background, they perform better academically and have more positive attitudes toward education.[11]

At the macro level, there are excellent examples of interventions that can be employed to close achievement gaps. Finland's success in building an excellent and equitable education system is well documented. Other countries could look to their universal access to early education that starts at infancy and the requirement that all public school teachers have a master's degree as proven ways to raise student outcomes.[12] Singapore's rise to the top of most world education ranking systems has been fueled in part by universal pre-kindergarten

---

11 The Effects of Teacher Match on Students' Academic Perceptions and Attitudes. (n.d.). Retrieved November 5, 2017, from http://journals.sagepub.com/doi/abs/10.3102/016 2373717714056?journalCode=epaa&

12 National Association of Elementary School Principals: Serving All Elementary and Middle-Level Principals. (2011). Retrieved November 5, 2017, from www.naesp.org/ principal-mayjune-2011-early-childhood/why-pre-k-critical-closing-achievement-gap

and decentralization of control in which regions were given increased autonomy.[13] A study published by *Principal Magazine* states: "The availability of preschool education is one strong predictor of differences in PISA (The Programme for International Student Assessment) scores across countries. In fact, institutionalized preschool education is found to increase school-appropriate behavior and cognitive abilities, both of which contribute to increased test scores." Countries looking to close gaps would be wise to invest resources in this area. Korea, Norway, Estonia and Hong Kong all are shown by PISA data to have among the most high-performing and equitable systems in the world.[14] All focus heavily on providing access to high-quality early childhood education to every child, regardless of background.

The general success of Canada's school systems is also well documented. From relatively mediocre world rankings on the international PISA test in the late 20th century, Canada has risen to be regarded as having one of the top education systems in the world since 2000.[15] Specifically, the province of Ontario has shone as a model for how a sustained focus on building relationships, meeting the needs of all students, and building the capacity of teachers can lead to increased opportunity for traditionally underserved children.

Since 2002, Ontario has seen 14 per cent more children graduating high school, an increase in math and reading outcomes, and the closure of achievement gaps for immigrant children, low-income students, and special education students.[16] An OECD case study attributes several factors to this dramatic improvement. Among the causes is a strong social safety net that helps children, regardless of family economic status, come to school ready to learn. Canada's belief that health care and other social services are a universal right carries over into education.

13 Organisation for Economic Cooperation and Development. (2010). Strong Performers and Successful Reformers in Education: Lessons from PISA for the United States (Rep.). Retrieved November 3, 2017, from OECD website: www.oecd.org/countries/singapore/46581101.pdf

14 OECD. (2013). *Are Countries Moving towards More Equitable Education Systems?* PISA in Focus, No. 25. Paris: OECD Publishing. http://dx.doi.org/10.1787/5k4bwpbqrz9s-en

15 Organisation for Economic Cooperation and Development. (2010). Strong Performers and Successful Reformers in Education: Lessons from PISA for the United States (Rep.). Retrieved November 1, 2017, from OECD website: www.oecd.org/pisa/pisaproducts/46580959.pdf

16 Fullan, M. (2012, May 4). What America Can Learn from Ontario's Education Success. Retrieved November 5, 2017, from www.theatlantic.com/national/archive/2012/05/what-america-can-learn-from-ontarios-education-success/256654/

Since children who do not have their basic needs met cannot learn, this safety net prevents children from traditionally marginalized groups from falling behind before they even enter the classroom.[17]

The culture in Ontario of teachers and families having high expectations for all students, regardless of immigration status was also cited as a reason for educational improvement. In fact, research seemed to indicate that the high expectations that immigrant families had for their children were having a positive impact on raising the expectations on native-born children from their families. These high expectations, when combined with a focus on allowing teachers the professional autonomy to innovate, provide avenues to spread successful pedagogies. At the same time, common sense professional accountability measures helped to spread academic success to most traditionally underserved populations.

All education systems have room for improvement. Not all equity gaps in Ontario and Canada's education systems have been closed. Recognizing the need to better serve First Nation children, Canada has focused in the last decade on the development of supplemental curricula to focus on indigenous history and pedagogical practices. Yet, First Nation children still lag behind others in their country on measures of academic achievement.[18] They have a graduation rate 36 points lower than Canadian students as a whole and are much less likely to attend post-secondary school.[19] Despite the obstacles, teachers are showing how a focus on community and developing individual relationships can help children in this population overcome the systemic headwinds they face.

Belinda Daniels is a teacher in Saskatchewan, and a First Nations member of Nehiyaw origin. Her students are active participants in social justice issues, including the preservation of cultures that have been maligned by colonial agendas historically pervasive in the Canadian education system. Studying indigenous culture, including history, language and shared oral storytelling gives her students the tools to resist the inequities they see in their own country, as well as parallel

17 Maslow, A. H. (1943). A Theory of Human Motivation. *Psychological Review*, 50(4): 370–96. doi: 10.1037/h0054346 – via psychclassics.yorku.ca.

18 Parker, S. (1970, January 1). Crossing the Cultural Gap: The Incorporation of Indigenous Pedagogies and Content into the Urban Classroom by Non-Indigenous Educators. Retrieved November 5, 2017, from https://tspace.library.utoronto.ca/handle/1807/77143

19 Wilkins, D. F. (2017). Why Public Schools Fail First Nation Students. *Antistasis*, 7(1): 89–103. Retrieved October 28, 2017.

issues that are apparent across the globe. Belinda's summer language workshop camps, started over a decade ago, provide opportunities for students to connect with cultural roots. Her dedication to ensuring students learn about all aspects of Canadian history, including that which is usually avoided in textbooks written by members of dominant cultures, has been recognized internationally. "Much work," she believes, "remains to bring balance, equality, and a respectful co-existence in our schools."

In Belinda's opinion, there is an urgent need to change the story of school, which is so often shaped by the dominant culture in a society. She states:

> I know that streaming our Indigenous students into categories of race or heritage is discriminatory. I know that the content of lessons has to relate to the student. I know that there needs to be more visible Indigenous educators and other Indigenous personnel involved in our schools. I know that sitting in rows and reading out of textbooks is killing the creative spirits in my students and, just as important, in me. Most importantly, I know that being in the moment, being spontaneous and fascinated about what is being learned in class, makes me realize that teaching has to be animated and alive.[20]

In Salluit, a tiny Inuit fly-in village in the Canadian Arctic, Maggie MacDonnell struggles to help her indigenous students overcome the significant challenges they face. Drug use, alcoholism, sexual abuse and teen pregnancy are rampant in the isolated and resource-deprived community. This has led to a suicide crisis that has taken the lives of many of her students.

Helping young people in her community overcome the disadvantages they face has become Maggie's life's work. Community building is at the heart of her methodology. The creation of a fitness center gave teenagers and adults in the village a place to de-stress and find a common activity. Taking students hiking through national parks led to activism to protect natural area. Having her students run a community kitchen allowed them to see how much good they could do for others and how much they each mattered.

20 Daniels, B. C. (2014, July). A Whisper of True Learning. *Learning Landscapes*, [S.l.], 7(2): 101–14. ISSN 1913–5688.

For Maggie, working toward a healthy community also meant dealing with difficult gender issues in Salluit. In addition to abuse and unplanned pregnancies, teenage girls often have to overcome the burden of domestic duties in their household, while trying to get an education. The life skills program that Maggie created, along with partnerships with daycare centers that provided mentoring opportunities, began to help young women see hope in their future.

The excellence of her work resulted in Maggie being named the winner of the 2017 Global Teacher Prize. Her message is now inspiring policy makers, politicians and other teachers to see the value of supporting efforts to close equity gaps, both inside and outside classrooms. While both she and Belinda are making incredible impact in Canada, their work can be used as a model to address complex equity issues in other locations.

Supporting Teaching that Closes Equity Gap

In the classroom, the pedagogical practices of teachers can serve to either increase or decrease inequalities among students. As we move further into the Fourth Industrial Revolution, it will be critical to spread best practices and professional knowledge to reduce inequality. A focus exclusively on academic achievement in our schools inherently widens gaps between those with sufficient resources outside of school and those who are disadvantaged. In a 2014 study, Laura Teague found that teachers who are under extreme pressure to produce better student test scores tend to utilize classroom practices that increase inequality. Students who are part of minority groups and already underrepresented or misrepresented in textbooks are frequently placed in low-ability groups in such situations, making it less likely that they will be able to overcome the racial, economic or gender disadvantages that led to their placement in the first place.[21,22] In order to avoid widening gaps, teachers must explicitly focus on supporting and understanding student backgrounds, meeting each student's individual needs rather than trying to standardize learning.

21 'Acceptance of the Limits of Knowability in Oneself and Others': Performative Politics and Relational Ethics in the Primary School Classroom. (n.d.). Retrieved November 5, 2017, from www.tandfonline.com/doi/abs/10.1080/01596306.2014.880047
22 Schools Are Harming Low-Ability Pupils' Chances by Teaching in Sets, Academics Say. (2017, September 4). Retrieved November 5, 2017, from www.tes.com/news/school-news/breaking-news/schools-are-harming-low-ability-pupils-chances-teaching-sets

Ginger Lewman, former teacher, founder of a Project-Based Learning (PBL) School, and author of *Lessons for Life Practice Learning*, believes
that developing a culture in which every student feels valued must
include intentionally fostering positive peer relationships. She explains:

> When the educational environment is able to move beyond the
> social pecking order hierarchy model and even beyond the 'every-
> one is the same' model, they've moved into the realm of what
> most people think is impossible: where each student accepts others
> for who they are and can appreciate each other's struggles for the
> benefit of the community.[23]

Tracy-Ann Hall, a teacher in Spanish Town on the island nation
of Jamaica, understands the need for a compassionate focus on each
student in her school. Her own experience as a student was not overly
positive, and her dyslexia, undiagnosed at the time, forced her to repeat
fifth grade. Becoming a teacher was never her ambition in her youth.
After graduating high school, she became an automotive technician
and worked in a garage.

Perhaps it was her own struggles that allowed her to understand the
needs of her students when she became a teacher years later. Her first
class was composed of 30 boys who had been written off by the system
due to their poverty. Tracy was determined to make sure that they had
a different experience in school than she had as a student. Through
a reading program and hands-on learning, those boys overcame the
negative perceptions about them and started to succeed. One of them
even became head boy of the school. The automotive classes she taught
achieved 95 per cent pass rates, and she developed partnerships with
businesses in the area, giving children in poverty the skills needed to
join the workforce and overcome economic challenges that were often
generations in the making.

Vocational training is also a key component of the curriculum at
EDventures academy in Bangalore, India, which, according to their
website was established to "provide educational opportunity to all children with diverse level of ability." Santhi Karamcheti, the founder of
the school, developed a groundbreaking program that works to increase
students' socio-communication skills and self-esteem in addition to

---

23 Lewman, G. (2016). *Lessons for Life Practice Learning: Because in School, We Want to Practice
Real Life, Right Now.* Hutchinson, KS: Essdack.

their academics. Students need to grow as individuals as much as accumulate knowledge. Each student has personalized goals that allow him or her opportunity to overcome limitations with which they may enter school. The success of these methods has received recognition from media and organizations around the globe, and the school's philosophy is now being viewed by others around the world as a way to help students with disabilities overcome their challenges.[24]

The common focus on individual students in the methodologies employed by Santhi and Tracy allows students to overcome the disadvantages they face. Their focus on Social–Emotional Learning (SEL) in addition to academics is critical to closing equity gaps. A 2017 report by the Aspen Institute and the Council of Chief State School Officers cites a focus on social–emotional development and school culture as critical components to a system in which every students' needs are met. According to the report: "Achieving equity means meeting the needs of every child, which includes providing a safe and supportive school environment, access to a well-rounded curriculum and appropriate technology, and regular examination of additional unmet needs."[25]

Within that "well-rounded curriculum," access to arts education is critical. This has been proven as an effective way to prepare students for school, work and life. Some of the skills that have been identified as vital for success in the Fourth Industrial Revolution are best taught through visual arts, music, dance and drama. Increased creativity in students who receive an arts–infused education is an obvious benefit. Research shows that communication skills, leadership, problem solving, civic engagement, perseverance and cross-cultural understanding are all developed in learning environments that emphasize the arts.[26]

The power of the arts to empower children was obvious to Kunle Adewale, an art therapist and Mandela Washington Fellowship for Young African Leaders recipient in Nigeria. His passion for his community drove him to develop programs that help children overcome the traumas of terrorism, illness and violent extremism through dance, drama and visual arts. By expressing themselves artistically, Adewale

24 EDVenture Academy Home Page. (n.d.). Retrieved November 5, 2017, from www.edventureacademy.com/

25 Arts Education Partnership. (2013). *Preparing Students for the Next America: The Benefits of an Arts Education (Publication)*. Washington, DC: Arts Education Partnership.

26 (n.d.). Retrieved November 5, 2017, from https://site.qudwa.com/en/media-center/white_papers/73/A-profile-of-tomorrows-quality-teaching

has helped over 3,000 victims of Boco Haram engage and reintegrate into their families and communities. Young women, who often face the most stigma, have particularly benefitted from his efforts which focus heavily upon developing a sense of belonging and community solidarity. Children dealing with autism, sickle cell anemia, Down's Syndrome and cancer have used Adewale's art therapy programs to reduce perception of pain, overcome loneliness and decrease stress. He has seen positive changes in the self-perception of those in his programs, including a marked decrease of depression.

Student-oriented practices which place the learner at the center of activities and give the student a more active role in the learning process, like those highlighted above, have also been shown to have positive effects on both motivation and learning. We need a shift in focus from accountability measures based on standardized test scores toward metrics that take into account universal access to quality teachers and learning environments, robust curricula that include the arts, as well as student engagement and wellbeing.

Helping our Next Generation Build a More Equitable Society

Many of the issues with which we are confronted in the Fourth Industrial Revolution will take several generations to overcome. Developing our next generation of action-minded global citizens within our schools will ensure our children have the means to create a better world than the one we are leaving them. We must strive for equity within our society while also building an appreciation for equity in our posterity.

Many teachers are using the United Nations Sustainable Development Goals (SDGs) as a foundation for developing global citizenship. These goals were adopted in 2015 to end poverty, protect the planet and ensure prosperity for all by the year 2030. According to Fernando Reimers, Director of the Global Education Innovation Initiative and the International Education Policy Masters Program at Harvard University,

> Education is not only one of the seventeen goals, it is also instrumental to the achievement of many of the remaining 16 goals, which include the empowerment of vulnerable people, the elimination of poverty, promoting physical and mental health, sustainable management of natural resources, fostering intercultural

understanding, tolerance, mutual respect and an ethic of global citizenship.[27]

Shortly after they were developed, a group of international teachers started a grassroots movement to bring SDGs into classrooms around the globe as a way of developing global citizenship. The Global Goals Educator Task Force is giving teachers resources, collaboration opportunities and inspiration to empower students as positive change agents in their society. Ada McKim is a Canadian teacher who was instrumental in starting the Task Force. She states: "It transforms what a classroom can look like when students have purpose that flows through their learning. The Global Goals can be connected to any aspect of any curriculum."[28]

In Vietnam, Global Goals Educator Task Force member Nam Ngo Thanh is determined to give his fifth-grade students opportunities to use their creativity to make the world a better place. At times, he has created projects based on the SDGs and invites other classes to partner with his students. In other instances, he has joined collaborative opportunities created by other educators in his online professional network. Through these projects and videoconferencing, his pupils have partnered with students on every inhabited continent to work towards solutions to water scarcity and pollution, gender equity issues and prevention of childhood sexual abuse. His students understand the need to develop creativity, grow as learners and apply the knowledge they obtain in schools as social innovators.

Robin Chaurasiya's female students in Mumbai come from one of the most marginalized populations in India. Many of them are victims of trafficking or children of sex workers in the Red-Light District. When they enter the Kranti School that Robin founded, they bring a variety of languages, ethnicities, castes, abilities and emotional issues. The school's goal is to help the girls overcome their backgrounds to become peer teachers and community leaders.

Overcoming inequity is nothing new to Robin. Her difficult childhood experiences in a family with a history of domestic violence

27 Reimers, F. (2015, September 15). We the Peoples . . . and the United Nations 70th General Assembly. Retrieved November 5, 2017, from www.huffingtonpost.com/fernando-reimers/we-the-people-and-the-uni_b_8120294.html
28 Global Goals. (2017, May 17). Retrieved November 5, 2017, from http://atlantic.ctvnews.ca/video?clipId=1126221&binId=1.1145745&playlistPageNum=1

and later expulsion from the US Air Force due to her sexuality have given her insight into helping her girls, the "Krantikaries," rise above the negative stereotypes they often face. Like the other examples in this chapter, the focus on the Kranti school is on meeting all of the needs of children rather than maintaining a narrow focus on academic achievement.

The Krantikaries are an incredible example of how education can be a tool to both help students rise above inequities they face in their community and become leaders that help others overcome marginalization as well. They have led workshops for over 100,000 people, delivered a dozen TEDx Talks to empower others, and successfully lobbied government officials to expand voting registration. Reciprocating the opportunity given to them has become a driving mission for these agents of social change.

The narratives from Robin's and Nam's schools show that learning is not a zero-sum game if children are empowered to use their learning to help others. When we provide excellent education to one group of students and utilize the technological tools of our time effectively, opportunity can be spread to others around the world. Compassionate innovation multiplies as it spreads. Education that meets the challenges of the Fourth Industrial Revolution should be designed to encourage empowerment of our next generation.

As we move forward, it is our moral obligation to give our children the knowledge, skills, competencies and empathy to overcome the issues they will face. At the same time, we must be careful to learn from the practices of teachers like Maggie, Belinda, Robin, Nam, Kunle, Tracy-Ann, Santhi and Inés, while also understanding that innovative teaching cannot overcome all of the inequities in our society. Teachers have incredible impact on students, but it is unrealistic to expect every teacher to innovate solutions to our collaborative problems the way these exceptional educators have. Our goal must be to celebrate these success stories and spread their impact.

Humankind has shown the ability to conquer incredible challenges when we utilize our collective resources and work toward a common purpose. There has not been a naturally occurring case of smallpox since 1977 because our global society decided we needed to eradicate a disease that was devastating to so many. Now, we must eradicate the inequities that threaten our future. Our collective will and focus must be upon ensuring each child on our planet has the education and opportunity to benefit from the amazing advances of the Fourth Industrial Revolution.

Through the efforts of their teacher, the children in Malawi mentioned at the beginning of this chapter are now seeing how this can be possible. Using social media tools and international networks that would have been impossible for a teacher in Malawi just a short time ago, Andrews Nchessie developed partnerships with teachers around the globe to help his children. He challenged students from distant locations to help solve the famine crisis his students faced. Through the collaborative fundraising efforts of schoolchildren on four continents, school gardens were created that allowed the Malawian children to both grow food and learn curriculum through gardening. A group of primary school students in Australia engineered collapsible chicken incubators that were used to help schools raise poultry for eggs. Community partnerships brought parents from the villages to the school to dig irrigation wells and help grow enough food to feed all students and sell surplus so that the gardens were sustainable.

Andrews's students are no longer missing classes to scrounge for food. Instead, their minds and bodies are being fed at school because of a project that could not have taken place a decade ago. They are preparing to be healthy, happy and contributing members of our global society. As technological innovation drives us forward, collaborations like this in which students use their learning to overcome equity gaps will be increasingly possible. It is up to us to make sure they become commonplace.

As Armand will demonstrate in the next chapter, in this era of technological change, students will need to be taught to be as adaptable and innovative as those in Andrews's class.

Chapter 4

Teach ME
The Learner Profile

Armand Doucet

Matt didn't like tests. He struggled to earn *B*s on written physics tests, which was odd considering the stuff he loved to do with his little brother at home. To avoid studying for those dreaded tests that made him feel stupid, Matt would take his brother's old toys, pull them apart and build new things. He would make an automated slingshot to fire at Jenga blocks and solar-powered blinds for their bedroom windows to rise at sunrise, made from bits and pieces of old toys and a solar-powered calculator. Matt was smart, but he was stuck in a system that only recognized a narrow definition of success for learners. The school system failed to support Matt and students like him, people who excel in competencies, but struggle with curriculum content.

Training students to be adaptable learners in this era of economic, social, environmental and technological transition will require a different set of assessment and teaching methods. To accomplish this, teachers must change how they teach and interact with students, abandoning their traditional role as classroom leader. Instead, they should adopt the mantle of guide and chief designer of a classroom culture focused on three foundational skills – literacy, competency and character. Key to accomplishing this professional transition, teachers will need to create personalized learning pathways for each student that recognize their unique abilities and challenges. This will require teachers to invest more one-on-one time in the first few weeks of the school year to get to know each student – an important step not only for building trust, but also for ensuring greater equity in the classroom. As we set out to design the Fourth Industrial Revolution classrooms, teachers need to be open to evolving their professional practice. This chapter provides an overview of core skillsets for the 21st century classroom and a practical guide for introducing new teaching methods, based on my experiences, the work at Riverview High School and examples from classrooms around the world.

My own experience supports the research that the 21st century classroom must prepare students for a world that will require them to be able to work collaboratively to solve unstructured problems and to effectively analyze information. These skills sit at the heart the World Economic Forum's (WEF) *New Vision for Education*, its 2015 paper produced in collaboration with The Boston Consulting Group.[1] It defines this trio of foundational skills in the following way:

- **Literacies**: how students apply core skills and foundational knowledge to everyday tasks. These skills and knowledge will serve as the base upon which students will build more advanced and equally important competencies and character qualities. The following are examples of foundational literacies:

  - Literacy and numeracy
  - Scientific literacy
  - ICT literacy
  - Financial literacy
  - Cultural and civic literacy

- **Competencies:** how students approach complex challenges. The following are examples of foundational competencies:

  - Critical thinking – The ability to identify, analyze and evaluate situations, ideas and information in order to formulate responses to problems
  - Creativity – The ability to imagine and devise innovative new ways of addressing problems, answering questions or expressing meaning through the application, synthesis or repurposing of knowledge
  - Communication and collaboration – Coordinate with others to convey information or tackle problems

- **Character:** how students approach their changing environment. The following are examples of foundational character traits:

  - Persistence
  - Adaptability
  - Curiosity

1 WEF & Boston Consulting Group. (2015). New Vision for Education: Unlocking the Potential of Technology. Retrieved October 15, 2017, from www3.weforum.org/docs/ WEFUSA_NewVisionforEducation_Report2015.pdf

- Initiative
- Leadership
- Social and cultural awareness

By 2030, this skillset will be commonplace in classrooms around the world, which will require new strategies, assessment, pedagogy and teacher education. Take computational thinking which is starting to be recognized as one of the most important competencies in the workplace; we definitely need to adapt to teach this in our classrooms.[2] Teachers, researchers and policy developers around the world recognize the need for this pivot, which has led to the development of multiple frameworks that use a different language to describe similar concepts and themes. In addition to the WEF, organizations such as the Organisation for Economic Co-operation and Development (OECD), the Partnership for 21st Century Learning (P21) and Canadians for 21st Century Learning and Innovation (C21), as well as numerous jurisdictions have sought to categorize the requirements of the 21st century classroom. For instance, "skills" and "competencies" are sometimes used interchangeably and sometimes defined as two distinct terms. For the purposes of this chapter, we have embraced the latter – skills and competencies are distinct. Taken cumulatively, these various studies and reports have identified five universal competencies: problem solving, collaboration, communication, creativity and critical thinking.[3]

These five competencies aren't just highly prized by educators to create an engaged and active global and community citizenship, but these are also the competencies needed for the Fourth Industrial Revolution workplace. Over the past half-century, the private sector has been increasingly involved in shaping our public education systems as employers and as sellers of educational products and services. This dual purpose is problematic for educational systems that do not have a clear vision and strategy for student learning and teacher training because it leaves them exposed to the influence of companies driven by self-interested profit goals, rather than societal needs. We must not give the keys to student learning to a few entrepreneurs, engineers and investors who are not professional educators. Silicon Valley's interpretation of what students need to be active and engaged in the world as

---

2 https://computationalthinkingcourse.withgoogle.com/unit
3 Sproat, L. (2015). Transformation and Technology in Education. *EdTech Europe*. Retrieved September 4, 2017, from www.slideshare.net/EdTechEurope/edtech-europe-2015-track-1-google-lizsproat

workers and as citizens is narrowly defined by their own workforce's needs. However, as educators, our responsibility is not solely to create the next workforce; it is to help raise the next generation of citizens. As philosopher John Dewey wrote in *The School and Society* (1899):

> The world in which most of us live is a world in which everyone has a calling and occupation, something to do. Some are managers and others are subordinates. But the great thing for one as for the other is that each shall have had the education which enables him to see within his daily work all there is in it of large and human significance.[4]

In his book *The Fourth Industrial Revolution*, Klaus Schwab challenges us "to create a framework for thinking about the technological revolution that outlines the core issues and highlights possible responses."[5] We need to ask the hard ethical questions in order to "create positive, common and hope-filled narratives, enabling individuals and groups from all parts of the world to participate in, and benefit from, the ongoing transformations."[6] We need to think about what education is at its core for each student. Is it, as Nelson Mandela stated, "the most powerful weapon you can use to change the world"? Or is it as Aristotle once defined it, as "the mark of an educated mind to be able to entertain a thought without accepting it"? Martin Luther King Jr. defined education's function as the requirement "to teach one to think intensely and to think critically. Intelligence plus character – that is the goal of true education." Our definition will likely draw from all of these and more. Out of this, we will build a practical framework to enable teachers to blend curriculum needs, social and cultural expectations and skillsets requirements into a new model for teaching and learning. In addition to the WEF's three foundational skillsets – literacies, competencies and character – we can also apply UNESCO's four pillars (4Ls):[7]

- Learning to know
- Learning to do

4 Dewey, J. (1899). The School and Society. Retrieved October 8, 2017, from https://brocku.ca/MeadProject/Dewey/Dewey_1907/Dewey_1907a.html

5 Schwab, K. (2017). *The Fourth Industrial Revolution.* New York: Penguin.

6 Schwab, K. (2017). *The Fourth Industrial Revolution.* New York: Penguin.

7 UNESCO. Retrieved October 14, 2017, from www.unesco.org/new/en/education/networks/global-networks/aspnet/about-us/strategy/the-four-pillars-of-learning/

- Learning to be
- Learning to live together

The challenge is to build these 4Ls into how teachers teach and address demand for literacies, competencies and character that our students need on a global scale. The goal is for a student to develop a reliable compass, the navigation competencies to find their own way through storms and strength of character to face volatile and ambiguous waters in order to survive.

I believe that teachers have always taught competencies and character. Many of us could learn from early childhood and guidance teachers, who do assess it and monitor student progress. Teachers of older students who are focused on content may not realize they were also developing competencies and character. I propose the Teach ME model, seen in Figure 4.1, that combines the WEF and UNESCO models. This model should be the foundation to designing your curriculum outcomes to address the whole child. This way when you are choosing to assess from projects you can also do formative assessment for character, competencies or the 4Ls.

The Teach ME model will help teachers design classrooms to prepare students for a world in which they will work and live among people of diverse cultural, religious and racial origins who may hold different worldviews. The Teach ME model provides teachers with a holistic

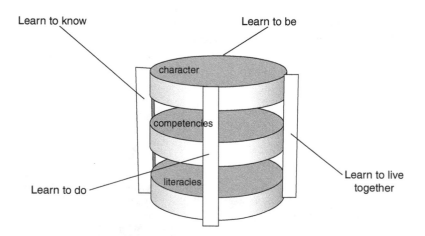

Figure 4.1 Teach ME model

approach to design student development, learning and assessment. The trailblazing teachers that have taken the previously mentioned skill-sets and made them their own which is what Dennis Shirley's states in, *The New Imperatives of Educational Change*,[8] as important to move education forward. What seems to work in the classroom is to engage students in competencies and character development via their interest and/or passions. We get to know individual students on a deeper level, meet them at what Vygotsky, a soviet psychologist who developed a sociocultural approach to cognitive development, calls the zone of proximal development, and challenge students' existing paradigms to help guide their development. We are just now considering the practicalities and realities of next steps, and many questions need to be asked. Furthermore, these frameworks should never and will never look the same across cultures around the world. The Teach ME model is presented as a starting point to help the discussion move forward within various jurisdictions.

The Teach ME model has driven my classroom practice. Without this model, a student of mine would not have been able to connect to her roots while in my modern history class. Conferencing with her, I realized that she really enjoyed music and was interested in finding out more about the story of her grandfather, a miner who lived through a disaster, who was showcased in one of the commercials for the Canadian Heritage series. Finding a connection to the curriculum through the social rights movement, I told her to go ahead with a personalized project (Passion Project, Chapter 6). She visited the mine which is now a museum and wrote a thesis connecting all the elements. For her presentation, she created a song from her grandfather's perspective which was as beautiful as it was haunting. Throughout this process, she was constantly self-reflecting and conferencing with me about creativity, collaboration and communication. She showcased resilience, grit and patience as she consistently prototyped her song to make sure it was to her standards. The Teach ME model is behind these projects and a reason why this student was able to have a voice.

While designing the Teach Me model, I was influenced by many teachers and their classrooms. One group of teachers really inspired me to believe that this model was feasible and worthwhile to construct. Engineering Brightness was created by three teachers Tracey Winey,

John Howe and Ian Fogarty to harness the potential of youth to impact authentic global problems. There are 1.3 billion people worldwide who suffer from light poverty, meaning they don't have access to light to study or read at night. By getting students to collaborate from around the world, they have created strong partnerships that are testing prototypes that could realistically solve this issue. These multi-aged students worldwide work with industry leaders, community members and students from developing countries to design a safe, hand-held, 3D printed, sustainable lantern. They link perfectly literacies, competencies, character and the 4Ls. Mechanical and electrical engineering skills are not only learned, but applied, and refined using the design thinking model. They learn how to collaborate, communicate, problem solve and create on a global scale. Global collaboration occurs by various means: Skype, country visits, guest speakers, email and hand-written letters. Every person involved in Engineering Brightness has learned how to be an engineer, philanthropist, and positive local and global citizen. Instead of just repeating physics on a worksheet, they have become physicists.

In the past, the education system has concentrated on the base tier (literacies = knowledge + skills), but this alone cannot prepare students for our changing world. As teachers, we all know students who have excelled at formal tests, but are decidedly unprepared for life's challenges and vice versa, such as Matt. Being book smart does not guarantee lifelong resiliency. This is the domain of competencies and character. To help students develop themselves to the fullest from K–12 based on the Teach ME model, here is a blueprint to start the discussion in your jurisdiction:

- Elementary schools (K–Grade 5): learning to do and learning to live together while building literacies and competencies with less focus on content learning
- Middle schools (Grades 6–8): character building, literacies and learning to be, connecting it to the community
- High schools (Grades 9–12): combine all of the above with learning to know, connect it to the larger world

Teachers have to do more than transmit curriculum content to students. They have to

- cultivate students' ability to be creative, think critically, solve problems and make decisions;

- help students work better together, by developing their ability to communicate, collaborate and be empathetic;
- build students' capacity to recognize and exploit the potential of new technologies; and,
- nurture the character qualities that help people have healthy lives, live and work together.

These demands on student learning in the Fourth Industrial Revolution have profound implications for both teachers and teaching. In addition to continuously updating their own knowledge of the subjects they teach, teachers are expected to work with multicultural classes, integrate students with special needs, be "assessment literate," work and plan in teams, assume some leadership roles and provide professional advice to parents. At first, many of these challenges seemed onerous, but by employing Dennis Shirley's *The New Imperatives for Educational Change*,[9] I have been able to gather insights from all these different frameworks to pivot my teaching. I have not copy pasted any of these directly into my classroom. By looking at best practices in these jurisdictions and what has worked for others, I created my own framework with ongoing research that works with my strengths as a teacher and the localized needs of my students. This will be elaborated upon in the personalized teaching chapter.

A Practical Guide to Introducing Teach ME into the Classroom

My practical guide to designing for the Teach ME model was first presented at lifelessonlearning.com[10] is a three-pronged approach that includes the creation of Culture, Design and Passion Projects for the classroom. This chapter will focus on Culture, Design and Assessment. Passion Projects will appear in Chapter 6.

Culture

To begin, we must create the right culture for growth and design thinking, which builds resiliency of character and the competencies of creativity, entrepreneurship and innovation. If teachers believe that their

---

9 Shirley, D. (2017). *The New Imperatives of Educational Change*. New York: Routledge.
10 Retrieved October 28, 2017, from www.lifelessonlearning.com

role is to foster personal development for each student, not dictate curriculum standards and are happy to relinquish some control, they can make my practical guide work. The education advisor Sir Ken Robinson says that, "the role of a creative leader is not to have all the ideas; it's to create a culture where everyone can have ideas and feel that they are valued."[11] I learn as much as my students throughout the year, collaborating with them to find solutions to the problems they embrace, finding experts to explain things they want to try or understand and seeking to make a difference in the world.

The examples of Maggie and Tracy-Ann that were used in Chapter 3 show that the creation of the right culture, based on getting to know the child first and foremost, will directly relate to student learning. Maarit Rossi from Finland understands that her students need to be connected to math instead of just doing worksheets. She proves that the subject can be stimulating and fun. Her students are often outside of the classroom learning from real-world settings. For her, math is a tool to make sense of the world rather than a list of rules. She creates the right culture understanding her students need for relevancy, engages them and empowers them to flourish.

The goal of this culture change is to encourage students to embrace the problems they face instead of fearing them. We use three actions to create the culture.

- Action 1 – Go Slow to Go Fast
- Action 2 – Challenge Paradigms
- Action 3 – Embrace the Problem

Action 1 – Go Slow to Go Fast, is partly based on the work of Dr. Sheryl Burgstahler,[12] which states teachers need to know students on a personal level and connect with them. Building relationships sits at the heart of my classroom work, especially in the first 3 weeks of the school year when it is done deliberately and formally. My students share their passions, likes, dislikes and issues in order to start building relationships. For instance, we use Multiple Intelligences and Meyers-Briggs

11 Robinson, K. (2006). Ted Talk. Retrieved September 29, 2017, from www.ted.com/talks/ken_robinson_says_schools_kill_creativity
12 Burgstahler, S. (2010). Universal Design of Instruction (UDI): Definition, Principles, Guidelines, and Examples. Retrieved September 2, 2017, from www.washington.edu/doit/universal-design-instruction-udi-definition-principles-guidelines-and-examples

Personality Traits test to begin to open up conversations with students about their learning processes. Mini-challenges are the order of the day, and I draw a lot of my inspiration from the summer camp icebreakers of my youth, such as the Lava Walk, egg drop challenge, paper to ceiling challenge, cup building contest and other easily set-up challenges. We drastically reduce curriculum coverage for the first 3 weeks, hence the name of this first action item Go Slow to Go Fast. The important part for teachers is to learn how each student reacts to these challenges, where they are in their social and emotional learning (SEL), who takes the lead, who follows, how they brainstorm and how they communicate. Often, divergent thinking, great ideas and creativity in collaboration are stifled at the brainstorming stages because of poor communication skills.

Australian teacher Christian Williams understands the importance of developing a culture of trust and safety in the classroom. When he was younger, he suffered from a lack of confidence and social anxiety, which was exasperated when he was diagnosed with a severe heart disability. The determination that he used to overcome his illness and represent his country as an international lacrosse player now drives him to give his students a more positive experience in school than he had. His use of athletic activities, experiential learning and community building to provide engaging lessons for children led to international recognition and being named a finalist for Young Australian of the Year in 2015 as well as a Top 50 finalist in the Global Teacher Prize 2016. Hanan al Horeb, 2016 Global Teacher Prize winner, used very different techniques to build the same culture of safety and nurturing in her Palestinian classroom. When she saw the way children in her village were affected by the violence they witnessed on a regular basis, Hanan knew she needed to find ways to help her students overcome their emotional trauma. She developed a program of teaching through play that allowed those in her care the opportunity to build social skills and positive relationships. Not only did her students feel safer, but their academic performance skyrocketed because of her nurturing.

Action 2 – Challenging Paradigms happens in Weeks 3 through 7 by overloading the students in different ways. At this point in the year, my students are being taught in one of two ways. Either they are being taught using a diversified pedagogy including old and new methods depending on their needs, or the students are fully engaged in the proposal/research phase of their Passion Projects, which I consider a curriculum extension. The students are purposely overloaded with tight deadlines to challenge their belief that they need to have the right answer. My goal is to get them to develop a more fluid, iterative approach to learning. At first, this can be traumatizing for high school students who already have a decade of being taught that the goal is a single, correct answer and are worried that failure will negatively impact their ability to get into the post-secondary institution of their choice. Students' character and competencies are largely challenged in this period, and they quickly realize that they are not confident in many of them. To help me understand what all my students are thinking, I encourage them to create video reflections in their digital portfolios, which allow me to monitor their development outside the time constraints of the school day. Often, issues arise in the video reflections that require both mini formal and informal conferences. If you know your students well and you do Go Slow to Go Fast properly, students will trust you to help them move forward.

Frustration happens when students get feedback on their skills and curriculum standards with no marks. Instead they get further questions which continue their development because I want to push against the belief that there is only one right answer or one way of doing things. The frustration is often felt by high-performing students as they have never faced obstacles at school. Facing obstacles challenges their resiliency, but is essential to combat the growing mental health challenges in the workforce. According to Tony Wagner:

> students who only know how to perform well in today's education system — get good grades and test scores, and earn degrees — will no longer be those who are most likely to succeed. Thriving in the twenty-first century will require real competencies, far more than academic credentials.[13]

For instance, the high school students in Brian Copes' engineering and technology class in Alabama are learning those real competencies. Combining service with practical application of knowledge, Brian's students have designed prosthetic limbs for patients in countries in the Global South who would not otherwise have access, and aquatic wheelchairs for members of his community. Recently, his students led a project that converted unused shipping containers into portable vocational technology classrooms for villages in Honduras.

---

13 Wagner, T. & Dintersmith, T. (2015). *Most Likely to Succeed: Preparing Our Kids for the Innovation Era.* New York: Scribner.

My classroom gives students a safe environment to face what they perceive as failure, or what I like to call a life lesson. This thinking is supported by Hattie[14] who says that evaluation (the giving of marks) and feedback, used separately, foster student success.

Action 3 – Embrace the Problem combines classroom growth and design thinking with the ability to self-reflect. Competencies and character development is integrated with the curriculum standards touching on the 4Ls. I become a guide in many settings. When I lecture, it is usually limited to the occasional mini-lesson, but each classroom is different depending on the needs of the students at that time. The diversified pedagogy in the classroom is often presented as mini challenges for individuals or groups depending on what we are doing. Consider the following two examples from my modern history class.

- Students created a mosaic that represented how they believed a soldier felt and how his senses were assaulted in the trenches during the First World War. Previously, a typical lecture would have lasted 1 hour, and I would have explored strategies, structure and a few stories from the trenches. Using a discovery based pedagogy with technology integrations, students came away with an understanding of 21 different topics including the animals living in the trenches, medical emergency procedures, censorship of letters, schedule, arms, strategies of war, unofficial peace stoppages, before and after look at the trenches, and the atrocities of trench warfare. They collaborated in small groups and as a class, and we had three students monitoring, negotiating and delegating at the front of the room. My role was to facilitate and ask probing questions to further their research. The personalized learning demonstrated throughout this activity, their personalized notes, and the assessment being personalized created a highly engaged learning environment.
- Students used our dry erase marker tables in small groups. They sketch-noted similarities and differences between the working conditions of children during the Industrial Revolution and their own world. Technology integration played a part here as students took pictures of their work, stored it and discussed it further

14 Hattie, J. (2012). Visible Learning for Teachers: Maximizing Impact on Learning. Retrieved October 12, 2017, from www.tdschools.org/wp-content/uploads/2013/08/The+Main+ Idea+-+Visible+Learning+for+Teachers+-+April+2013.pdf

in their different chat groups which fostered Learning to Live Together, communication and collaboration.

I spend an enormous amount of time building the right classroom culture to enable a growth mindset and foster divergent thinking, using Actions 1, 2 and 3. It is important that students trust me and believe in where I, as the teacher, am guiding them because trust is the root for fostering the foundational literacies, competencies and character.

On the first day of class, a very shy kid walked into my class. He could not answer a direct question in front of the class, turning beat red. After building a relationship and fostering trust over the first few weeks, he started to open up a bit, specifically in his video reflections. I could see he was very passionate about architecture, had a love for new technology and interested in books. Connecting all of these, he did a project comparing Nazi architecture to the architecture in the capital of the fictional book *Hunger Games*. It was simply amazing with him 3D printing small-scaled building to showcase during his presentation. He stood up in front of the class and presented an hour-long talk. Furthermore, he had the opportunity to present at ISTE and Princeton University.

When I was teaching middle school, a group of teachers and myself created a Harry Potter week. We completely transformed the classes, school culture and school activities to have Harry Potter at the center of everything. Curriculum outcomes were taught by using Harry Potter as the content. We got students to try and figure out how to make brooms fly for our flight unit. In English class, students created alternative endings to the first book. We had a Quidditch World Cup in physical education. Schoolwide, we ran a Daily Prophet, Triwizard Cup, Wizards chess and TriWizard Ball (dance). The schoolwide decorations, pedagogy, activities and running commentary online garnered over 1.8 million views. It created a worldwide network for our students to interact with giving them the opportunity to develop the 4Ls. The key was that every learner profile and staff member participated in creating Harry Potter week.

Design

The design of my high school modern history course is built with competencies and character development fully integrated with the delivery of curriculum standards (literacies) using a flexible structure. To accomplish this, I must be able to pivot quickly based on how students are moving through the content and skills, the state of their Passion Projects and the emerging needs related to these projects. I am less involved in their projects once students embrace the problems and are comfortable self-reflecting and networking. The conversations become about "how to" instead of "what am I doing wrong?" This aspect of the class is often misunderstood and misinterpreted in non-education circles. This type of student-centered approach pushes the development of civic and global literacies by giving them democratic solutions and making students active participants in their learning. Using our Teach ME model, teachers can plan to teach for the whole class or for individual students personalizing their approach to each student. In order to avoid overwhelming students, it is helpful to work with your colleagues in the school to address student needs and avoid the risk of them burning out.

Assessment

Character, competencies and the 4Ls matter and should be formatively assessed throughout a student's school years. Can these traits be quantified on a report card? Camille A. Farrington, a researcher at the University of Chicago, says there are so many ways to do this "wrong" and that "in education, we have a great track record of finding the wrong way to do stuff."[15] Assessing character, competencies and the 4Ls doesn't mean we need to quantify it. Musicians, athletes and artist improve dramatically through qualitative formative feedback.

Attempting to quantify character, competencies and the 4Ls by putting in a single number on a report card, is exactly how we could get this wrong.

> Reformers today, by and large, believe student successes should be carefully tested, with teachers and principals receiving better pay if their students advance more quickly and get canned if they fall

15 Zernike, K. (2016). Testing for Joy and Grit? Schools Nationwide Push to Measure Student's Emotional Skills. *New York Times*. Retrieved August 28, 2017, from www.nytimes.com/2016/03/01/us/testing-for-joy-and-grit-schools-nationwide-push-to-measure-students-emotional-skills.html

behind. . . . Standing from their soap boxes, it is easy for outsiders to critique what teachers do in the classroom and base student success on test scores which would be completely missing the point on education.

Khan[16]

The talk around the world is about competencies and character, but the truth is that teachers and parents do not see this on the report card and educators are taken to task for results based on test scores for curriculum content. The pressure felt by teachers to meet curriculum content has overshadowed moves towards teaching the development of competencies, character and the 4Ls. In an attempt to bring credibility to developing the whole child, students have long received grades for behavior-related categories like citizenship or conduct. However, rating implies that character is singular when, in fact, it is multifaceted and our feedback on these traits is insufficient and unclear. So, I give constant feedback to my students by using digital platforms that permits me to stretch the school day. Instead of having my students for 60 minutes and trying to fit as many conferences as possible, I am able to conference or leave each of my student's feedback every night or when the need arises. Platforms that give me the opportunity to share video, pictures and voice with the student and parent, while also giving us the opportunity to discuss growth and place to improve, is critical for my practical guide to work.

This digital platform to me is key because it gives the chance for students to have a voice when often they would not speak up at first in class. A student of mine, who had been constantly late on assignment in most of his classes, arrived late with an assignment early in the semester in mine. We conferenced in-class with mostly me telling him he could do better. He did not share his thoughts, he was too shy. When he got home, he sent me a video selfie and explained that he needed to work full time because his dad was very sick and his mom was having addiction issues. A student in high school working a full-time job and making great grades. Knowing his social-emotional state, I let him negotiate extensions to the assignment. He never missed one deadline that was negotiated together. Without the digital platform, I don't believe he would have advocated for his rights.

16 Thompson, C. (2011). How Khan Academy Is Changing the Rules in Education. *Wired*. Retrieved August 29, 2017, from http://southasiainstitute.harvard.edu/website/wp-content/uploads/2012/08/Wired_2011-8-HowKhanAcademyIsChangingtheRulesofEducation.pdf

Angela Duckworth is a global leader on researching grit, one of our character traits. She worries she has contributed, inadvertently, to an unpalatable idea.

I vigorously oppose high-stakes character assessment. New federal legislation (United States) can be interpreted as encouraging states and schools to incorporate measure of character into their accountability systems with nine California school districts starting to do so this year.[17]

How do you quench the thirst for standardization while meeting the goals of teaching to the whole child? The literacies are summative and are included in high-stakes testing with the goal of standardization and accountability in education. However, if we truly want to be aligned with the vision of developing competencies and character of our students, education needs to re-think high-stakes testing in literacies. Like Dennis Shirley asked in his book do we want standardization and accountability or achievement with integrity?

New Imperative for Educational Change teachers[18] are empowered to design assessment models creating that balance. My fellow Riverview High School teachers Chris Ryan and Ian Fogarty[19] have developed a model of essentials and extensions to balance the learning of content and skills within literacies. Mastery of the essentials gives space to develop and assess character and competencies. It is critical to assess the character and competencies to move a student forward despite it not being recorded in a report card. It is given as written and conversational formative feedback.

The students need strategies when it comes to developing character and competencies. Teachers and parents also need guidance in how to help them. Here are some great examples of activation strategies for this feedback, when by asking students to

- explain how they solved a problem;
- apply what they have learned to new contexts;

---

17 Zernike, K. (2016). Testing for Joy and Grit? Schools Nationwide Push to Measure Student's Emotional Skills. *New York Times*. Retrieved August 28, 2017, from www.nytimes.com/2016/03/01/us/testing-for-joy-and-grit-schools-nationwide-push-to-measure-students-emotional-skills.html

18 Shirley, D. (2017). *The New Imperatives of Educational Change*. New York: Routledge.

19 Fogarty, I. & Ryan, C. (2017). Bringing Assessment Research to Practice Using an Essentials Model. In J. Cummings & M. Blatherwick (Eds.), *Creative Dimensions of Teaching and Learning in the 21st Century*. Boston: Sense Publishers.

- learn from mistakes;
- solve problems in several different ways;
- answer questions that challenge students to reflect on how to solve problems;
- question what they believe is true; and
- apply their competencies and character in different situations.

Teacher Education

For this new practical guide to work, society must trust the professionalism of teachers, and teachers must hold each other accountable.[20] The education system needs to invest in adequate training to pursue the development of character, competencies and the 4Ls. We recognize that the professionalism embedded in the Finnish education system is something that we should all be striving to achieve. Finland treats teachers as white-collar workers on the same level as doctors; in many parts of the world, teachers are group of semi-professionals who need to be constantly monitored and supervised – much like the traditional view adults have of children. I don't think it's luck that the Finnish system is celebrated because they are very much part of the New Imperative of the teaching profession by Dennis Shirley, which touches on all five elements.[21]

Currently, teachers are graduating with well-developed skills to teach literacies; they lack the tools to teach the rest. Teacher education institutes must adapt in order to prepare new teachers for a different classroom environment, one that embraces interconnectedness of teaching literacies, competencies and character. Also, professional development for teachers already in the classroom must be addressed and scaled accordingly. In some places around the world, university graduates without a Bachelor's of Education get a minimum amount of training and are placed into some of worst neighborhoods and are expected to make a difference because of their content expertise alone. I believe you are sending lambs to the slaughter. Yes, some will thrive, but only because they are naturally gifted educators. However, for true mastery, you need experts in content, as well as pedagogy, social work, guidance and psychology.

20 Shirley, D. (2017). *The New Imperatives of Educational Change*. New York: Routledge.
21 Adamson, F. (2016). Privatization or Public Investment in Education. Retrieved October 17, 2017, from https://edpolicy.stanford.edu/publications/pubs/1456

UNESCO predicts that there will be a shortage of 69 million teachers worldwide by 2030.[22] It will be extremely tempting to fill this gap with technology and minimally trained people who will transfer knowledge in its most basic form to our students. Instead, we should have professionals who understand the art and science of designing personalized pathways to develop character, competencies, 4Ls and literacies. With the proper time and facilities, we can build a model to support countries struggling to educate or attract quality teachers.

Applied and experiential learning should be better integrated into teacher education, perhaps opening up the opportunity for greater collaboration with post-secondary institutions. In some places in the world where there are 150 students in a classroom, a single good quality professional teacher who can contextualize the learning is better than five or six untrained educators.

The irony is not lost on me that society needs to be as concerned about the education of our teachers as we do about the education of our students.

In a time where some jurisdictions are returning to classical education of Latin, and where technology threatens to automate content delivery, it is critical to set our eyes upon preparing the whole child, with all of their intricacies, home lives, talents, passions and hopes to enter the Fourth Industrial Revolution. As Nadia will demonstrate in the next chapter as she examines successful education models around the world, teachers need to evolve from simply delivering traditional knowledge towards designing lessons that develop literacies, competencies and character.

> The spirit of our times places certain obligations or 'imperatives' upon all educators. The very term 'imperative' may be disconcerting to those who privilege choice. But choice should not be its own end. It should serve higher purposes. Choice is easy. Imperatives are hard. But the greatest educators have never ducked the challenges of their age. They have confronted them with courage and fortitude.[23]

22 UNESCO. Retrieved October 11, 2017, from www.un.org/apps/news/story.asp? NewsID=55210#.WgCpnI9SzIU
23 Shirley, D. (2017). *The New Imperatives of Educational Change*. New York: Routledge.

Chapter 5

The Power of Teaching

Dr. Nadia Lopez

It is a hot day in June, at last check, the temperature is 87 degrees, but in a vast, brightly lit, non-air-conditioned auditorium with over 400 people, it feels more like 100 degrees. It is a proud moment for me as my fifth graduating class at Mott Hall Bridges Academy, a middle school located in Brownsville, Brooklyn, makes their way down the aisle swaying from left to right in unison with great pride – statistically they should not have made it this far. The energy is electrifying and contagious. We have all gathered for this joyous occasion to witness these graduates, whom I affectionately call scholars, from Mott Hall Bridges Academy, make history as they prepare to enter a new chapter – high school. In the 3 years, the many who came in reading on a third-grade level, will now read ninth-grade level books, learn robotics, pitch a business plan, and know how to deliver a TED Talk. This is all possible because of the hard work and dedication of the teaching staff committed to providing a quality education that prepares our scholars to navigate the 21st century.

In September 2010, I opened Mott Hall Bridges Academy (MHBA), a middle school, in Brownsville, one of the most underprivileged and crime-ridden communities in New York City. With high unemployment and dropout rates, the average income, according to the 2010 US Census, in the housing projects is a staggering US$ 11,000. Only 32 per cent of residents have a high school diploma, 14 per cent earned a bachelor's, and 3 per cent have obtained a master's degree. In 2016, according to the New York State standardized assessments, 88 per cent of our incoming sixth graders were below a third-grade level in reading and math. Nearly 32 per cent of our scholars classified with special education needs, with an additional 35 per cent who we have identified as being at risk. While the data presented academic gaps, the other challenges we face were the social-emotional needs that became exacerbated by mental health issues that have gone untreated. Our teaching staff, which is comprised of 33 per cent new teachers from alternative teaching programs with less than 3 years in education, and another 33 per cent previously worked in failing schools where they did not receive professional development or instructional feedback.

Drawing from my own personal experience of becoming a teacher through an alternative teaching program, I quickly realized how unprepared I was to deal with seventh-grade students in the Fort Greene section of Brooklyn, who were reading below a third-grade reading level. Learning education theories with teacher-centered models, rather than actually practicing student-centered approaches, had not prepared me for a classroom environment with limited access to technology, the pressures of standardized testing, a rigid curriculum that was responsive to updates in policies rather than changes in society, and a lack of professional development personalized to meet my needs as a new teacher.

The transition from working in a corporate setting at Verizon, the telecom company, to being in the classroom made me realize the disparities that exist in our school system. Teachers require an adequate education that will prepare them to teach the next generation for the 21st century. We must design curriculums that are responsive to the exponential effects of automation, global demands and new emerging markets that represent the fusion of technologies of physical, digital and biological industries. Innovation requires constant reskilling. Thus, building knowledge of the content, incorporating the use of technology, and cultivating soft skills such as active listening, critical thinking, problem solving, adaptability and collaboration will be essential in the Fourth Industrial Revolution.

Greatness in the Classroom

In Jim Collins's book *Great by Choice*, he states "thriving in a chaotic world is not just a business challenge . . . but about the principles that distinguish great organizations from the good ones."[1] While the global education system has yet to ensure that all nations are able to meet the demands of the 21st century, throughout various classrooms, you will find great teachers who go above and beyond the call of duty to create learning experiences that reflect our ever-changing times. Unsatisfied with settling for mediocrity, great teachers are noticeably the individuals who put in extra hours to work with students after school, plan

---

1 Collins, J. (2014). *Great by Choice*. New York: HarperBusiness.

lessons, grade papers, facilitate an extra-curricular activity, serve as a mentor to their colleagues or just simply decorate their classrooms. They understand the importance of knowing each of their students, personalizing their learning, and dedicating time to discover alternative ways to best support each student's needs. As devoted lifelong learners, they seek opportunities to learn how to improve their craft, collaborate with colleagues, and share their experiences and knowledge. Great teachers are passionate about their teaching and learning; hence they believe in the power of education and the implications it has on a child's development for the future.

When I entered the field of teaching, Julia DeCoteau was my mentor and co-teacher. She was a brilliant educator who showed me the importance of developing an adaptive teaching style and the value of personalizing students' learning. I recall vividly on the first day of school she had created baskets of reading books that ranged from picture books to chapter books like *Breathe Eyes Memories* by Edwidge Danticat for high school students. Every child was given the opportunity to select an independent book and was expected to read daily for 30 minutes during the class reading time. One particular young lady named Candace selected a picture book, as did many of her peers. While reading, she struggled and wanted to give up, because she was too embarrassed to continue. After class, Ms. DeCoteau asked Candace to stay and told her that she would be willing to stay after school with her to get through the book without any distractions in the classroom. She wanted Candace to know that it was okay to read on a lower level, but that the goal would be for her to eventually read on or above her grade level, by the end of the year. For many of our colleagues, it was hard to believe that within a year Candace, who was academically on a second-grade level with an individualized education plan and being raised by her maternal grandmother, would be able to achieve such an ambitious goal, but she did. For 8 months, Candace stayed after school to work in a small group that allowed her to get the support she needed. With each passing day, Candace began to build confidence in her reading and her improvement became noticeable in her other classes. She went from reading picture books to chapter books, then eventually writing essays that were minimum 9 pages long. At the end of the year, Candace had increased scores significantly on the English Language Arts standardized exam, and she began talking about wanting to go to college.

Fast-forward to 2017 and Ms. DeCoteau now works for me as my seventh-grade English teacher in Brownsville where the demographics is similar to the Fort Greene community. Despite their low achievement, our children are called scholars to create a mindset that they are lifelong learners who are preparing for college and future careers. In 14 years, Ms. DeCoteau's teaching style has evolved significantly after she had the opportunity to travel the world for a couple of years, taking some time away from teaching. Her travels led her to visit schools in other countries in the Caribbean and on the continent of Africa; the experience moved her to incorporate the global citizenship into her instruction to cultivate empathy, exploration and collaboration beyond the classroom.

In her non-fiction unit, Ms. DeCoteau made the scholars read the book *I am Malala*, which they resisted reading at first. However, being methodical with her approach, she would build on the scholars' prior knowledge and cultivate their critical thinking skills through classroom dialogue and project-based activities. An interdisciplinary curriculum that incorporated lessons on geography, religion and patriarchal societies gave scholars the opportunity to explore how people could be marginalized based on geographical location and gender inequalities. The inclusion of TED Talks, news reports and guest speakers who had firsthand knowledge of Malala's culture further deepened the scholars' understanding, which developed their empathy towards another culture. Socratic seminars conducted throughout the reading of the book encouraged scholars to engage in text analyses, to build critical thinking skills and learn how to effectively communicate their ideas to their peers.

For the completion of the end-of-unit performance task, scholars used Google Chromebooks to write an argumentative essay in their Google Docs, which they shared with Ms. DeCoteau. By using this digital platform, scholars enhanced their technological skills and could receive feedback in real time to edit their writing. Not only did Ms. DeCoteau evolve in her practice as a teacher, but she has been able to cultivate the technological and soft skills that scholars will need to throughout their academic and future careers.

Models of Success

Let us look a little closer at the Finnish system of education, which we have touched upon in previous chapters. In Finland, there is less emphasis placed on using standardized testing, to rank students and schools, there is high investment in selecting the best teaching candidates to complete a robust teaching preparation program that requires practicing the delivery of instruction model school, observing a master teacher, and receiving ongoing feedback from faculty or supervising teachers.[2] The rigorous process of selecting hundreds of prospective teachers from thousands of applicants requires each successful candidate to achieve high scores on a college entrance exam, demonstrate effective communication skills on a written exam, and articulate their passions and reason for becoming a teacher during the interviewing process.

Through their rigorous education, teachers are expected to use a holistic approach to know their students and understand their capabilities to provide them with the support services they need. Both special education and general education teachers are highly qualified and learn to effectively differentiate their instructions to meet the needs of all the students in their class.[3] This is extremely beneficial, considering that nearly one-third of students, while in early education, are identified with special needs or at risk in areas of mathematics, reading and writing. Additionally, Finland provides an equitable distribution of funding for all students to receive a quality education no matter their socioeconomic status, race or gender.

The approach implemented by Finland schools is reminiscent of Johann Heinrich Pestalozzi, the Swiss education reformer known as the Father of Modern Education. In 1774, he opened the Neuhof School, welcoming children with different learning abilities and talents, varying in ages from 4 to 17. He found that even the weakest students could thrive if provided with a stimulating learning environment. Although the school closed in 1779, Pestalozzi believed that "true education goes hand in hand with human nature; it touches heart, spirit, and hand."[4] In his forward-thinking approach, he used personalized learning to meet students where they were at and customized their experience based on their needs. Like Finnish teachers have been taught, this approach requires an understanding of each students' strength and their weaknesses. For Pestalozzi teachers have the power to encourage a child's natural curiosity and motivate them through hands-on experiences. Through real-world situations, they begin to

2 Sahlberg, P. (2013). Teachers as Leaders in Finland. *Education Leadership*, 71(2): 36–40.
3 Morgan, H. (2014). Review of Research: The Education System in Finland: A Success Story Other Countries Can Emulate: 453–7. Springer Science and Business Media.
4 Laudback, M. & Smith, J. (2011). Educating with Heart, Head, and Hands: Pestalozziasm, Women Seminaries, and the Spread of Progressive Ideas in Indian Territory: 342–56.

form language and understand relationships between things in their environment.

We have mentioned PISA (The Programme for International Student Assessments) in previous chapters. It is a standardized exam, administered every 3 years to 15-year-olds. It is used to measure math, reading and science. Unlike nations such as the United Kingdom and Singapore that use the results to rank their schools and students, in Finland, it is considered a low-stake exam. Ironically, in comparison to their counterparts, Finnish students' outcomes are considerably higher, but the assessments are only used as a tool for professional development to train teachers on how to analyze data to measure students' growth and provide them with feedback.

With less time in the classroom, teachers have more time to plan their lessons, collaborate with their colleagues, and explore the world beyond the school building to share their experiences.

Disrupt the System

Singapore has been recognized for having the highest ranking in student achievement measured by the TIMM (Total Impact Measurements and Management) and PISA assessments, but its success comes from the high quality of teachers who are selected from the top third of their high school graduates. Seen as belonging to a noble profession, teachers can earn as much as US\$ 77,693 and retention bonuses ranging from US\$ 10,000–US\$ 36,000 every 3 to 5 years, after successfully completing an intensive evaluation process.[5] Additionally, there are three pathways for teachers to pursue: teacher track – become a master teacher; leadership track – training for a position in leadership; specialist track – conduct research and develop policy. Professional development is ongoing and required, with a minimum of a hundred hours per school year for teachers. School leaders attend a management through the NIE (National Institute of Education) and have the opportunity to participate in a leadership exchange program that allows them to travel abroad to further develop their skills and deepen their global perspective.

Singapore also has an ongoing process of self-improvement and demonstrates a willingness to learn from other successful models that it is able to apply to its own education system. It has taken an innovative

5 National Center on Education and Economy. Retrieved from www.ncee.org

approach to driving internationalization, which fosters a deep commitment and sense of urgency to equip all of its students with the skills, competencies and drives to succeed in competitive global workplace.[6] Its number one priority is to remain relevant and learn from successful models that are above the curve in education. When Singapore sought to find the best practices in physical education, arts and culture, senior educators and the Minster of Education from Singapore, traveled to New Zealand, Australia and China to find models they could replicate. They then designed a framework that established several teaching academies dedicated to the improvement of physical education, arts and music. Institutes like NIE prepares all in-service teachers for the entire school system. Teacher education begins with pre-service that requires teachers to maintain values to stay abreast to what is happening in the real world to prepare them for the challenges their students will have to face in the Fourth Industrial Revolution. There are three core values known as V3Sk (Values, Skills, Knowledge), which focus on[7]

• Putting the learner at the center of the teachers' work and knowing how they learn best
• Being responsive to students' needs and maintaining high standards and strong drive during rapid change in education
• Committing to working collaboratively and becoming a better practitioner

Teachers design a curriculum that is responsive to the changing landscape of society that keeps their content and technology current. This reflects the national needs of Singapore and prepares students for the exponential changes occurring as a result of the Fourth Industrial Revolution.

In the Spring of 2017, the Board of Education in Gyeongsangnam-do province in South Korea visited Mott Hall Bridges Academy with a primary focus to observe project-based learning in a disadvantaged community. According to OECD PISA 2009 database, South Korea ranked first in in reading and in math,[8] yet as a high-ranking successful

6 Lee, S. & Low, E. (2011, March). Bringing Singapore's Teacher Education Beyond Its Shores: 43–51. New York: Springer Science and Business Media.
7 National Center on Education and Economy. Retrieved from www.ncee.org
8 Tan, O. (2011, March). Fourth Way in Action: Teacher Education in Singapore: 35–41.

school district they considered our project-based learning model as one that could be replicated within their classrooms. The opportunity-fostered collaboration between the South Korean teachers and our school opened up the dialogue about the delivery of instruction that is influenced one's culture. Overall, the experience demonstrated that education can build bridges across the globe, and we can learn from one another, especially in the interest of finding the best models to educate our children.

Gender Biases in the Teaching Profession

While Singapore and Finland continue to attract their best talent for the teaching profession and offer a substantial salary compared to other countries, according to the report *Women and the Teaching Profession: Exploring the Feminization Debate* published in 2011, there is a higher percentage of women compared to men who teach in the primary grades. While males outweigh females in secondary education, many women feel that they are steered into the early childhood years. The report points out that primary teachers are expected to be female by "parents, school principals, and society in general, because the teacher is a substitute mother and will be more caring towards the child."[9] A female focus group that was surveyed shared further that for many their parents encourage them into teaching because it was more suited to raise a family and culturally suited for girls. There was little opportunity given to consider other professions such as engineering or computer science that are male-dominated fields of study.

Many males view teaching as limiting their upward mobility and lacking the prestige of professions like law, medicine and business. There are other reasons why there are disparities between the numbers of men seeking to enter the teaching profession, compared to women. One, females outperform males in school making them less qualified to become teaching candidates. The low-paying salary makes it unattractive to seek or stay within the education field. Stereotypes create social biases that perpetuate the notion that teaching is for females, rather than males.

In one of his well-known books *Leinhard und Gertrud*, published in 1781, Pestalozzi, referenced women who played a significant role in

9 OECD. Retrieved from www.oecd.org/pisa/pisaproducts/pisa2009database-download abledata.htm

his life; for him women represented maternal characteristics required in teaching.[10] His work became a great influence in the training of women entering the teaching profession during the 19th century. In 1826, Mrs. C. M. Thayer governed the Elizabeth Female Academy in Mississippi, where she taught the Pestalozzian methods emphasizing sensory experience, reasoning and intellectual development. Pestalozzi's progressive philosophy and moral education spurred more female seminaries to open offering education that was just as challenging as men's and caused reforms from the United States to Europe.

We need to be aware of the gender biases that exist in our curriculum and the materials distributed throughout our classrooms. As Alex Harper, a Varkey Teacher Ambassador has pointed out,

> I often pondered as I worked through the endless pages of algorithms in my *Betty and Jim* textbook, why Jim always got things right and was obviously smarter than Betty. Gender stereotyping was strongly prevalent in the hidden curriculum. Today this is lesser the case. Saying this, gender should remain a topic of focus to benefit both boys and girls.

In the country of Samoa, females tend to outperform their male counterparts in pursuit of the Pacific Senior School Certificate, which qualifies them for entry into the Diploma of Education. This has been an ongoing trend happening throughout many countries in the world, resulting in fewer male candidates. For those who taught, but decided to pursue another career, they have verbalized that as the breadwinner, their low salary made it impossible to survive and provide for their family and see a brighter future for himself or herself.

In an interview with Jim Tuscano, another Varkey Teacher Ambassador from the Philippines, he concurred that the profession of teaching in his country should provide better compensation. As he stated: "Filipino teachers, earn a basic salary of about P20,000 per month [roughly US$ 400], that's without tax and other deductions yet. In order to elevate interest in teaching, we should change policies such on compensation." Our candid conversation revealed how qualified candidates can become dissuaded from becoming a teacher because

---

10 Laudback, M. & Smith, J. (2011). Educating with Heart, Head, and Hands: Pestalozziasm, Women Seminaries, and the Spread of Progressive Ideas in Indian Territory: 342–56.

there is no incentive to working long days, in possibly an overcrowded classroom, only to make a minimal amount of money.

Despite the shortcoming of the salary, Jim shared the improvements he has witnessed in the teaching profession,

> I had the privilege to work in one of the progressive schools in the Philippines and I have seen how 21st century skills are being developed in students. The improvement in teaching has then made student learning more focused into skills mastery. Students are more confident in learning. In a special way, my involvement in school initiatives such as the integration of iPad or mobile devices in learning has improved learning and student engagement in particular, in my students, as shown by the data and studies I have led.

A Pedagogical Shift

According to the World Economic Forum White Paper Report, *Realizing Human potential in the Fourth Industrial Revolution: An Agenda for Leaders to Shape the Future of Education, Gender and Work,* there needs to be an investment in the development of teachers to ensure they cultivate curiosity, collaboration and critical thinking skills in teachers.[11] As industries experience change, with some jobs becoming obsolete, while new ones emerge, it will be imperative to educate children on these skillsets and instill the values of becoming lifelong learners that will be necessary to navigate through the Fourth Industrial Revolution.

> While the profound uncertainty surrounding the development and adoption of emerging technologies means that we do not yet know how the transformations driven by this industrial revolution will unfold, their complexity and interconnectedness across sectors imply that all stakeholders of global society – governments, business, academia, and civil society – have a responsibility to work together to better understand the emerging trends.
>
> Klaus Schwab, *The Fourth Industrial Revolution,* p. 2[12]

As globalization increases, the need for students to become well equipped with skills that will prepare them to work in new and

---

11 World Economic Forum. Retrieved at http://www3.weforum.org/docs/WEF_EGW_Whitepaper.pdf
12 Schwab, K., (2017). The Fourth Industrial Revolution. Penguin, 2017.

existing industries is reliant on the capacity of teachers. Therefore, partnerships must be developed between education institutions and private organizations to give access to existing markets and those that will be emerging, to have a better understanding how the skills taught will be applied beyond the classroom. In Grenada, the University of Saint George's, which is recognized internationally for its medical program, has invested in the development of teacher leaders and school administrators by hosting an annual Principals Forum. Realizing that many of the schoolchildren who apply to university are not prepared to handle the rigor of college, the Department of Educational Service organizes this event for over a hundred educators and government officials to come together and engage in professional development feedback sessions which address the needs within the education system. The university's willingness to become a resource to educators, is an investment to benefit students and communities of Grenada so they are better prepared and have more options for their future.

As Dennis Shirley stated in his book, *The New Imperative of Educational Change: Achievement with Integrity*, "achievement with integrity means engaging with the wider world beyond one's own borders as a classroom teacher and as a constant learning professional."[13] The presence of Artificial Intelligence is fueling the debate on whether it will replace teachers in the classroom; the use of apps and digital platforms have in many cases become favorable to the personalization of learning. But it cannot, as Schwab eloquently states in his book, "lift humanity into a new collective and moral consciousness based on a shared sense of destiny." In other words, technology is opening doors and empowering children to build their knowledge, but it's humans who teach the development of skills that will allow our students to become global citizens that use their knowledge to collaborate with others to solve both local and global issues. Cultivating lifelong learners who are able to adapt to new technologies, workplace innovations, and self-motivated professionals.

Through a learning centered approach, the needs of students can be addressed while including interest and builds skills. As John Dewey once stated: "Knowledge, in other words is the product of an adaptive process of engagement. Adaptation in its most basic definition is a negotiation between existing core values and relation and changing

---

13 Shirley, D. (2017). *The New Imperatives of Educational Change.* New York, NY: Routledge.

circumstances."[14] He believed if students learn the skills to critically think, collaborate, and communicate with a diverse population of stakeholders, they would become productive citizens equipped to deal with the future even in uncertain times.

While automation within the Fourth Industrial Revolution continues at an exponential rate, it is evident that the use of technology within the curriculum must be incorporated as a tool that supports learning within the classroom and creates opportunity that extends beyond communities. The phenomenal work that Koen Timmers, fellow co-author, is doing by connecting communities around the world through digital platforms that allow students to collaborate and share their project-based activities on climate change, is defying limits that once existed because of physical boundaries. He will demonstrate his groundbreaking work in Chapter 7. Education reformers like Pestalozzi and John Dewey understood that teachers were vital in preparing children for the future. When we teach girls that they can be entrepreneurs, architects, computer scientists and engineers, then we begin to dismantle the stereotypes that limit them from pursuing any and every career. It is not just about preparing students for a particular workforce, but to also become agents of change that have a positive influence within humanity.

Standardized testing should be used to evaluate where children are at in their learning, but should not be used to penalize schools or incentivize progress. As Armand will demonstrate in the next chapter, we need to develop a more personalized approach to education; our assessments should take into consideration that children learn differently and come in to schools on various levels, therefore adopting a more holistic approach to measuring their individual progress will be essential.

If the vision is for all children to be prepared for the 21st century, then the mission must begin with education reform. It is important that governments implement education policies that reflect the programming, preparation and development of technological skills students will need to be successful at in navigating the future. Also, the teaching profession must be valued, by offering higher salaries that

14 Tarrant, S. & Theile, L. E. (2016). Practice Makes Pedagogy: John Dewey and Skills–Based Sustainability Education; and World Economic Forum. (2017). Realizing Human Potential in the Fourth Industrial Revolution: An Agenda for Leaders to Shape the Future of Education, Gender and Work.

will increase retention, offer professional growth and add prestige to the career. Investing in the continuous education of school leaders and teacher preparation programs will be pivotal in the assurance that all children receive the highest quality of education, no matter their gender, geographical location or socioeconomic status.

Chapter 6

Contextualizing Personalization in Education

Armand Doucet

The Syrian refugee crisis entered my classroom in the arms of a teddy bear. I teach modern history at Riverview High School in the Canadian province of New Brunswick on our country's East Coast. In 2016, Canada agreed to welcome thousands of Syrian refugees, almost all of them sponsored by community groups. They arrived with little knowledge of English or of the northern environment they now found themselves in. While many in our school empathized with our newly arrived neighbors, one of my students decided to act. Each semester, I instruct my students to create and implement a semester-long project around something they are passionate about that connects to curriculum outcomes. We call them Passion Projects, and this particular student elected to do something to help Syrian children refugees. She wrote and illustrated a children's book about a teddy bear who was experiencing the same trauma and anxiety as the refugee children in order to build empathy with elementary students in Moncton. To create the book, she researched the emotional and psychological effects of World War II's British child refugee crisis and compared it to the current Syrian refugee crisis. In doing so, my student learned new skills, developed competencies, deepened her understanding of world events and explored how to connect with an audience through creativity – all essential learning outcomes for students readying themselves for a world in economic, social and political transition.

People have unique skills, abilities, strengths, desires, paths and futures. Most of us don't want to believe or feel that we are part of a factory line learning environment. Hence a movement towards personalization in education, with its tag lines of autonomy, pace and choice. The belief is that students are expected to move through material together and don't have a say what they learn. The education system should be driven by students' own interests and inquiry intertwined with the demands imposed by teachers, schools and communities.

Schools have timetables; learning does not. The past decade has ush-ered in a generational shift in the way people consume, process and use information. Adults and students can choose how much or how little information they receive, and they can also choose how deeply they want to engage and influence real-world outcomes. As teachers, our role has been changing as well, from purveyors of information to guides on the learning journey.

There are many competing interpretations of what personalization is – and is not. How personalization is enacted will depend greatly on one's perception of education and value system. The key is to focus on a whole-child curriculum versus a high-stakes accountability sys-tem that incentivizes teaching to the test. We do need accountability in our education system, but not to the detriment of what is actually happening in our classrooms. Bi-partisan politics should not influence education, but it should be what is best for the child, which is often a balanced approach. These binary conversations and unethical use of data to push an agenda of saving or making money off education, is extremely damaging. We need to protect our classrooms and stu-dents from "educational" companies and politics that sometimes are more concerned about the bottom line versus the whole child. As teacher professionals, we need to do our due diligence before bringing things into our classrooms. The pendulum should not swing from one view to another frivolously, but stay relatively in the middle. Being in the middle would mean that we are looking at the whole perspective, exactly like a teacher does every day in a classroom when they feel supported by the system to do what is best for the child and not the bottom line.

Dennis Shirley of the Lynch School of Education, Boston College, identifies achievement with integrity as the new imperatives of edu-cational change.[1] He advocates adapting personalization models to the specific strengths, weaknesses and context of the local education sys-tem. No system around the world should be blindly duplicated as this disregards local cultures, institutions and political systems. Personaliza-tion needs to grow organically from within, using a model such as our Teach Me model in Chapter 4 as a guide.

Personalization in education is a loaded term. While personaliza-tion is accepted in the Finnish Model, elsewhere its definition has been co-opted by various movements, each seeking to bend it to a narrow

---

1 Shirley, D. (2017). *The New Imperatives of Educational Change.* New York: Routledge.

definition that is really standardization in disguise. For instance, our current embrace of technology in and of itself is not what personalization is all about. Even if, it does answer the catchlines of autonomy, choice and pace. Sticking a laptop in front of the student and giving them the opportunity to work on a particular school subject while tackling the scaffolding done by an Artificial Intelligence (AI) is not personalization. It is a system based on accountability and standardization forgetting the most important part of personalization, which is connecting and contextualizing the learning to develop the whole child. According to Adamson, part of the reason why the Finnish model is celebrated is because "Finland focus on the principles of equity, creativity and the 'joy of learning' that produced their high-quality systems in the first place."[2]

Context is key when it comes to personalization, and it will look very different depending where you are in the world. For instance, in Canada, I have the opportunity to personalize learning via individual student Passion Projects that connect personal interest with the curriculum). In contrast, my Ugandan teacher friend has a context vastly different than mine. She would find it difficult to have Passion Projects for each of her 150 students, even with the help of technology. In her context, personalized learning will be based on the realities of her students' lives and what is happening in the community. Her job is to connect how the students can impact outcomes at the local level, similar to what Andrew Nchessie demonstrated in Malawi (Chapter 3). In both instances, curriculum core knowledge will be learned, but the development of skills, competencies and character can be done via group or individual projects.

As technology, and in particular Artificial Intelligence (AI), becomes more influential in society, we must ensure that all citizens have the foundational knowledge, literacies, skills, competencies and character traits to be productive contributors to society, such as seen in our Chapter 4 Teach ME model. Technology will play a critical role in providing teachers the tools for a humanistic personalized education.

Personalization can help develop character, competencies, skills and core knowledge for each individual, including teaching students how to live and work together. It is important to help students flourish into their own individuals; however, we need to balance individual liberty with the need to be good global citizens and a good neighbor if our world is to survive. Personalization can strike that balance if done properly; however, it will widen the inequity gap if done poorly. We see this already with children in well-off areas getting opportunities to develop the competencies necessary to survive in the Fourth Industrial Revolution, while others don't have the same access.

When Wemerson da Silva Nogueira began teaching, he faced a school crisis. The poverty and drug use in his town in Brazil, along with a lack of student motivation, had driven the dropout rate to nearly 50 per cent. He realized that his teaching needed to speak to the particular needs of his students to motivate them to attend school and learn. Building a sense of community was vital, so Wemerson turned to the Rio Doce, a heavily polluted river regarded as an environmental catastrophe by residents. Wemerson had his students run chemical studies on the river in the school laboratory and interview members of the town to see how the river could be cleaned. After partnering with the laboratory at the University of Espirito Santo, the students began leading a clean-up project. The end result was that students were motivated to attend school and prepare for their future because of Wemerson contextualizing their education properly. Graduation rates went up dramatically, while drug trafficking and violence in the school dropped by 70 per cent.

Personalization in education is not new. It is how Socrates taught Plato, and it sits at the heart of John Dewey's constructivism. However, within today's reform movement in education is a push for this "new" personalization in education. A popular narrative from these reformers is that our current education system is a relic of an older age, born of the Industrial Revolution's need for an assembly line workforce that required people to follow a repetitive, routine, compliant work shift, punctuated by the labour bell. Their purpose was to largely ensure the momentum of the assembly line and assemble bureaucrats who could keep it going. Only a selective few ended up in creative, non-routine, collaborative jobs. While this is indeed true, this narrative has been co-opted and over-simplified to justify educational reforms that, rather than a rethinking of education, are merely the continuation of the industrial model of education, this time controlled and defined by Silicon Valley's very specific requirements. This school of thought undervalues the role education plays in the development of core literacies, competencies and character. The people that argue for personalization based on the need to pivot from this Silicon Valley model narrative do so in order to make a particular point about their vision for what learning could be like, which is often without a teacher. These sort of sketches and catchphrases never capture the complex history of educational practices or institutions. Education writer Audrey Watters continues that much of

> personalized learning is imagined and built and sold by tech companies by metrics, marketing, conversion rates, customer satisfaction using different words such as outcomes-based learning and learning analytics. This is the Silicon Valley narrative, an ideology that draws heavily on radical individualism, libertarianism and is deeply intertwined with capitalism.[3]

We need to ask ethical and moral questions of education's place in society. Disruption for disruption sake is not the answer. The Silicon Valley narrative will pivot our education system, but it's a dangerous crossroads steeped with dangers at every turn.

There is truth in these interpretations. The education system does need to prepare students with the skills to adapt quickly to the ever-changing nature of digital hardware, digital networks, digital information and digital collaboration, as defined by Université de Moncton researchers Mario Chiasson and Viktor Freiman.[4] At the same time, Audrey Watters cautions against identifying ed-tech as "the savior to all our problems in education because it's new, different, disruptive and above all necessary."[5] Without great pedagogy, technology integration is worthless especially for competencies and character.

For me, personalization in education should be implemented, not because it is the latest fad, but rather because it is the best thing for students. EdTech can free the teacher to create, innovate, deliver to students and track student progress, but it needs to form a supplementary role to well-designed classrooms that use multiple great pedagogies that touch on our holistic Teach Me model (Chapter 4) to meet all the students' needs.

3 Watters, A. (2017). Audrey Watters Blog: The Histories of Personalize Learning. Retrieved October 22, 2017, from http://hackeducation.com/2017/06/09/personalization
4 Chiasson, M. & Freiman, V. (2017). Closing the Gap: How Can the School System Embrace the Age of Acceleration? Retrieved September 12, 2017, from http://mariochiasson.com/wp-content/uploads/2017/07/proceeding_178369-1.pdf
5 Watters, A. (2017). Audrey Watters Blog: The Histories of Personalize Learning. Retrieved October 22, 2017, from http://hackeducation.com/2017/06/09/personalization

The Myth of Personalization

Teachers know one-on-one tutoring is effective. In 1984, the education scholar Benjamin Bloom figured out precisely how effective it is through a meta-analysis of research on students who'd been pulled out of class and given individual instruction. Bloom determined students given one-on-one attention reliably performed two standard deviations better than their peers who stayed in a regular classroom. What country can afford one-to-one tutoring full time? Perhaps some can, if it is automated. Herein lies the personalization through technology myth – that educational success will be achieved not through human attention, agency or policy. Rather, it will be achieved through computing technologies. Technology and resources to automate the delivery and assessment of certain literacies, specifically literacy, numeracy and science literacy already exist. There are databases of videos, digital worksheets and self-grading assessments. There are multiple perceived advantages to using these resources such as:

•   Automation brings a standardization of the perception of the transfer of knowledge, based on a lecturing pedagogy.
•   Automation answers the public's demand for accountability in education, which is reasonable given the implications for society.
•   Automation can provide the necessary foundation of knowledge that every individual will need to have in order to be a productive member of society.
•   Automation reduces costs by eliminating the need for teachers, infrastructure and layers of bureaucracies.

Now, the lowest hanging fruit to automate education is to standardize the transfer of knowledge. However, this is a model purely based on validity of the transfer of knowledge, a check mark on a bureaucrat's checklist. It has nothing to do with an education system based on achievement with integrity which would connect literacies and skills to competencies and character. Basically, it simplifies education to a one-trick pony of stand and deliver. It is both laughable that decision makers are thinking technology can work on its own without teachers, and frightening that it is not seen as just another tool for teachers to use with great pedagogy.

Within this myth, the belief is that the most obvious method to reconcile the push for personalization with accountability, foundational learnings and standardization is to provide a linear path in a variety of disciplines. For instance, in many subject areas from math to visual arts, there is a natural progression from one topic to another. At first glance, a teacher could be replaced by a video database that holds the knowledge, followed by some automated digital worksheets and a self-grading assessment. Students will have choice on which discipline to pursue first, and the pace at which they progress.

These sort of predictions and assessments about the present and the future, frequently serve to define, disrupt, destabilize our educational institutions, casting doubt about teachers' ability to perform as professionals. Decision makers feel the pressure to push for further account-ability and standardization through policy which continues a vicious cycle of teaching to the test and pushes teachers farther away from teaching to the whole child.

At its extreme, students on individual "personalized" paths could be placed in cubicles with a security guard rather than a teacher. Students come in, plug in, information is fed to them, they take a test and they plug out, go home and repeat. This is a superficial implementation of personalization. They are still on two linear paths, the first selects the knowledge path, and the second selects the technological tool upon which to travel. This entire process can be automated, standardized, and evaluated, which is attractive for policy makers and very profitable for business. In the end, all students follow similar paths. While they use the right buzzwords, it is a slippery slope to dehumanized education and has nothing to do with personalization.

Watters argues that EdTech has always been more "Thorndike than Dewey because education has been more Thorndike than Dewey. That means more instructivism than constructivism. That means more multiple-choice tests than projects. That means more surveillance than justices."[6] However, EdTech is now being rebranded as personaliza-tion and by extension, as progressive education.[7] Much of the EdTech world argues teaching machines could personalize and "revolutionize" education by allowing students to move at their own pace through curriculum. Watters uses a quote by Pressey that the automation of the menial tasks of instruction would enable education to scale.[8] I don't

6 Watters, A. (2017). Audrey Watters Blog: The Histories of Personalize Learning. Retrieved October 22, 2017, from http://hackeducation.com/2017/06/09/personalization
7 Watters, A. (2017). Audrey Watters Blog: The Histories of Personalize Learning. Retrieved October 22, 2017, from http://hackeducation.com/2017/06/09/personalization
8 Watters, A. (2015). The Automatic Teacher. Retrieved September 14, 2017, from http://hackeducation.com/2015/02/04/the-automatic-teacher

disagree with this statement as many tasks a teacher does in his everyday workload could be automated. However, this is a small part of the overall teaching profession, and it would not revolutionize the pace. Many teachers are already getting students to move at their pace and finding a variety of ways to give students agency over learning connected to the curriculum. The art of identifying students' individual interests, needs, beliefs etc. and finding ways to give each individual agency over learning in a way that meets those individual nuances is the reason that robots could never replace teachers. That process requires empathy and compassion for students, balancing everything that is happening to truly get to the learning, which is something algorithms cannot do. It is the art teaching that truly personalizes learning by adding choice, autonomy and pace to connect the curriculum to the students in different ways.

Some jurisdictions and charter schools are already employing models without looking at the whole perspective of education or the different elements that educators teach. Thinking you are an expert versus really being one is important to clarify for the education profession. With the state of our world today and the critical role of education in ensuring the future success of our society, relying on alternative facts is not an option.

Ethical Personalization in Education

In the near future, the private sector's biggest priority will be decreasingly about trade and increasingly focused on the challenge of retraining workers. If personalization is done right, students will head into the workforce with the competencies, character and a strong foundation of literacies to be able to pivot when their jobs warrant it. The Fourth Industrial Revolution will exacerbate inequities in jurisdictions that don't personalize learning well. Can EdTech help? Definitely. Will it be because it replaces teachers in the classroom, I surely hope not. Personalization is about connecting students' passion to the curriculum, but it is also about diagnosing a child's academic, social and emotional needs and using that knowledge to help them grow in ways they might not have known were even possible. We are professional teachers because we have the ability to map out development and the tools to make it happen for the whole child including core knowledge, skills, competencies and character. One who is excelling academically may need to be challenged in order to provide opportunity to build resiliency that will be critical to his or her future success. Resiliency is a skill that will be highly needed during the Fourth Industrial Revolution. Personally, I have seen way too many students who fail after their first semester at university because they have never developed the skills to overcome being challenged.

Academic pressure is very high in Hong Kong, with deleterious results on students' mental health. Ronnie Cheng of the Diocesan Boys' School (DBS) in Hong Kong has paved the way in trying to take a more rounded approach to education – focusing on the journey of learning as well as the results in examinations. He has given appropriate and measured support to students while still being one of the top schools in Hong Kong. Ronnie's has developed a #1-world-ranked male choir, winning many international championships over the last few years with many students have gone on to become professional musicians. However, he has never lost sight of each student wellbeing while pushing his students to strive for excellence.

For the possibility of personalization to exist, it needs to be more than just students using technology and teachers pivoting their practices. Education also needs leadership to align strong design, vision and strategy. The Organisation for Economic Co-operation and Development (OECD) states that

> powerful learning environments will constantly create synergies and find new ways to enhance professional, social and cultural capital with others. It will do this with families and communities, higher education, cultural institutions, businesses, and especially other schools and learning environments.[9]

A way forward for personalization will include environments in which great classroom pedagogy is infused seamlessly with relevant educational technology. According to the OECD,

> this knowledge of teaching and learning refers to the specialized body of knowledge concerned with creating effective teaching and learning environments for each and every student. It includes, for example, knowledge of how to structure learning objectives, how to plan a lesson, how to evaluate a lesson; knowledge of effective use of allocated time and strategies for differentiated instruction

---

9 www.oecd.org/publications/teaching-excellence-through-professional-learning-and-policy-reform-9789264252059-en.htm

and knowledge of how to design tasks for formative assessment. The knowledge also includes specialized areas of learning, such as knowing how to facilitate learning given certain student characteristics, such as their prior knowledge, motivation and ability level.[10]

In a small rural town on the coast of Maine in the United States, Beth Heidemann's kindergarten students don't let their young age stop them from having a huge impact on their local and global communities. For Beth, respecting each child as an individual and developing relationships are at the heart of her teaching. She claims:

> Belonging must come first, as young children can only be open to change and challenge when they feel safe, loved, and respected. I create innovative methods and tools that nurture a strong sense of belonging and inspire curiosity in my students. My home visits and deep relationships with families humanize an educational system that has left many families feeling disenfranchised and excluded.

Each year, Beth spends the first few months figuring out the passions of her students. Then, she uses all of the resources at her disposal to develop lessons and experiences that allow her "Cushkins" to learn through those passions. One year, a Skype call with children in an African slum resonated with her kids. During the call they recognized a parallel between the food insecurity in their community and the challenges the children in the slum faced. Beth helped them research the issue. Then, the children wrote a fairytale set in Africa that explained the issue of hunger. After they illustrated the book, Beth helped them publish it, with proceeds going to the local food pantry.

Another group of students was passionate about taking things apart and building them together again. Beth saw this as a great opportunity to teach them about engineering and recycling. Throughout the school year, they would collect record players, small appliances that were broken, and other materials. First, they would make predictions about the former uses for those items. Then, they would take them apart and use the design process to create something new. They became so

---

10 www.oecd.org/publications/teaching-excellence-through-professional-learning-and-policy-reform-9789264252059-en.htm

passionate about this project that a guest speaker who came to their classroom toward the end of the year was shocked when he showed them a picture of a road strewn with garbage. He had expected them to be appalled at the garbage, but instead the children became excited to see a road full of items they could retool into new creations.

Every student around the world has building blocks of knowledge that need to be developed from reading, writing and basic math. Some of this could be personalized. Why are early childhood kids in Africa or indigenous students in North America only reading colonial stories when they have a rich literary history that would make it more relevant to their context? As you progress, you will be exposed to many other cultures, but in your early years, shouldn't you be able to see yourself in stories?

Indigenous students who are able to learn in their native language see great benefits to self-identity and learning outcomes. Papahana Kaiapuni is an indigenous language immersion program that was established as an attempt to revive Hawaiian language after a century-long ban was lifted. Those who went through the program showed high levels of proficiency in both the English and Hawaiian languages. Perhaps more importantly, students and teachers who participated in the program developed a stronger sense of personal identity.[11] With suicide being the leading cause of death among young indigenous people worldwide, this focus on positive self-identity is critical.[12]

Belinda Daniels, a teacher Michael features in Chapter 3, struggled herself in school as a student of Nêhiyâw descent. She says:

> When I think back to being a student, I realize I still suffer from the emotional scars I endured, such as discrimination and the feeling of not belonging there. I do not think those feelings ever go away, no matter how much time has passed. My urban high school years were not filled with joyful memories, and not at all like you in the movies like *Pretty in Pink* or *The Breakfast Club*. They were filled more with awkwardness, isolation, and alienation.[13]

Now as a teacher herself, Belinda works to make sure her students never have to face the same isolation. She helped develop a high school

11 www.tandfonline.com/doi/abs/10.1080/15235882.2000.10162774?src=recs
12 http://assets.survivalinternational.org/documents/1438/progresscankill.pdf
13 www.learninglandscapes.ca/index.php/learnland/article/view/653/653

curriculum for Core Cree with the Ministry of Education of Saskatchewan, and initiated a bilingual Cree elementary program to give students the opportunity to have a much more positive experience in school than she did as a child.

An authentic personalization learning experience should have multiple components. A few of the requirement for teachers is to have a knowledge of

- their global and local community;
- each student and their individual learning paths;
- how to develop students' social emotional and competencies;
- the curriculum content and how to connect it to students via diversified pedagogies and strategies;
- learning and career pathways unknown to the student;
- a network inside and outside the school to collaborate in and enhance the students learning; and
- how to encourage students to reach beyond their comfort zone.

Teachers and students create personalized learning plans that take all of this into consideration. While autonomy, choice and pace are wonderful attributes to personalization, failure consider other equally vital aspects of the learning process can lead to disaster. It is not a free-for-all with students coming to school with a checklist of content that they need to meet to the exclusion of the rest of our Teach Me model. Teachers use their students' passions and strengths to explore ways to help students overcome areas of weaknesses or uncomfortableness. This is what personalization is all about.

A Model (Based on My Work with lifelessonlearning.com)[14]

A personalized education must balance the need for critical learnings with the desire to explore personal interests, hobbies and passions. This requires a teacher plan that blends essential teachings with what I and my fellow teachers at Riverview High School call learning extensions. The essentials are the components, standards or what we call literacies/skills of the curriculum that must be mastered by all students and are taught using a variety of old and new pedagogies, depending on the needs of the

14 www.lifelessonlearning.com

students. The extensions allow teachers and students to delve more deeply into curriculum as well as explore divergent topics, interests or passions. This facilitates a more personalized path driven by student engagement. The extensions concept was developed by Riverview High School staff.[15] The essentials vs. extensions model is driven by these questions:[16]

- Does it develop student readiness for the next level of learning?
- Is it essential for success in the next unit, course or grade level?

With this model, the extensions become the driver for developing and fostering the scaffolding of competencies, character and a growth mindset. Teachers play a large part in disseminating the curriculum into essentials and extensions. It is up to the classroom teacher and their professional learning community to discern the details of what is essential and how they are taught. The scope and sequence of the curriculum essentials is done with diversified pedagogy to match student needs as well as competencies and character development planning.

The essentials are a method to ensure students have a depth of fundamental literacies and skills in a particular discipline and in a manageable size. This allows students to work at their own pace and show their learning in a multitude of ways ranging from tests, thesis, observations and conversations. The amount of work is reasonable for almost all students. Time is variable; the learning is constant. The essentials ensure a foundational amount of knowledge with some choice, autonomy and pace. After the minimum requirements of the curriculum are met through essentials, extensions are possible to allow students to see their true potential as learners and global citizens. Passion Projects are a great way to make this happen.

Passion Projects[17]

The purpose of my Passion Project is threefold:

- To personalize student learning

15 www.learntechlib.org/p/172791)
16 Reeve, J. (2002). Self-Determination Theory Applied to Educational Settings. In E. L. Deci & R. M. Ryan (Eds.), *Handbook of Self-Determination Research* (pp. 183–203). Rochester, NY: University of Rochester Press.
17 www.lifelessonlearning.com

- To empower students to chase their passions in a design thinking and growth mindset
- To further develop competencies and character

These three components are the most important factors required to engage students' personal growth. Passion Projects become play as students take complete ownership of their learning. Each project is set up using the design process which includes Discovery, Interpretation, Ideation, Experimentation and Evolution in a loop format; students in my class prototype the three aspects of the project at least three times. It starts with the teacher finding out about student passions (Action to Culture 1 – Chapter 4) and talking with students to discover possible ideas. Once they are ready, students create a 3-minute proposal/ elevator pitch in their chosen medium. The three prototypes and final product consist of an oral component based on storytelling, a creative piece (think museum piece) and an academic thesis.

The Passion Projects allow students to choose an aspect of the extension curriculum content and link it to a passion of their own. Personalizing the content, owning their learning, and creating something genuinely unique in a design thinking process touch the four strategies that Marzano, Pickering and Heflebower[18] outline for engagement:

1   Use effective pacing.
2   Demonstrate intensity and enthusiasm.
3   Build positive teacher–student relationships.
4   Use effective verbal feedback.

Students take ownership of their Passion Projects, which means teachers must relinquish an aspect of the traditional teaching toolkit: how students are evaluated. If the goal is to have competencies and character developed as well as curriculum standards, you need to co-construct with students rubrics for the Passion Projects. Students will develop expertise in content and will be given complete latitude in their presentations. Also, they are given any medium to do their creative part of the project, but with some structure that changes for each student depending on the medium and student need. Students become stewards of their time, with the opportunity to negotiate different deadlines depending on their progress or situation. They network and

18 www.marzanoresearch.com/resources/tips/hec_tips_archive

collaborate with their peers and experts all over the world in many different subjects beyond modern history to help them with all aspects of their projects.

A female student passionate about math explored the possibilities in my modern history class by researching the role of women played at Bletchley Park in helping to break the Enigma machine codes. In particular, she became fascinated with Mavis Batey who is now a hero of hers. To showcase some of the frustration felt at Bletchley Park, the student designed an obstacle hunt based on her created code machine which the students need to break to get clues.

By working directly with others to change outcomes, students learn how to see the world through a variety of perspectives, often different from their own. This is an essential skill for our increasingly interconnected world. How do we teach empathy in education? Reimers describes this need in his first interdependent dimensions of the Global Competencies. For instance, in addition to the storytelling project, a second of my students also looked at the Syrian refugee crisis, this time from the perspective of yoga and its interaction with social rights. This student wanted to see how they linked together. After talking with me, she decided to look at the history of refugees from the Jewish diaspora during and following the Holocaust to the African refugee crises in Rwanda, Somalia and Sudan. That research led her to conclude that reintegration into society can cause anxiety and stress in the children. She decided that she wanted to help. She created a yoga instructional video with Arabic subtitles so that refugees could practice yoga with their peers and build friendships in an inclusive environment that reduced stress and anxiety.

Passion is what engages and empowers students; that is the driving force in my Passion Projects. Teachers all over the world have also figured out that harnessing students' passions humanizes education and develops the whole child. Grammy-nominated New York City-based teacher, Melissa Morris, uses music to help her students bridge cultural gaps. Music is another way to build empathy and cultural understanding. Through drum circles and world music studies, her students have gained appreciation for the histories and customs of people from every inhabited continent. That appreciation has grown into collaboration over time. Her students became so passionate about showing how music could bring people in distant locations together that they worked with children in Mexico to put on a live, two-country concert. Through videoconferencing, students harmoniously shared songs for audiences in both locations, and others who were watching live from other places in the world.

Personalized learning is more than a few catchphrases and cool technologies. In order for personalized learning to fulfill its potential, the entire system needs to be thoughtfully aligned with the focus on students learning to know, do, be and live together. We need changes to the timetable, school structure and assessment policy. A base level of literacies must be achieved as a foundation so students can chase their passions. Those core literacies and skills within them should continue to be sought as they go through their whole schooling. Each student is important enough to have learning contextualized and connected to their lives.

OECD states that building deep, conceptual understanding and higher-order thinking requires intensive teacher–student interactions, and poorly implemented technology distracts from this valuable human engagement.[19] Furthermore, teachers need to become better with the kind of pedagogies and management of time-environment for students that make the most of technology.

Joe Fatheree, mentioned in Chapter 2 by Elisa, is such as teacher, who has leveraged technology giving his students the opportunity to create award-winning documentaries on par with those being created by professionals in the film industry. He has seen the benefits of connecting students to people in industry and business while leveraging technology in the classroom to enhance their learning. Through these partnerships, Joe's students have shown that students do not have to wait for graduation to apply skills competencies and knowledge learned in school; they can get started in the midst of their school experience. His students work to address issues in their community such as poverty, bullying and homelessness. His students are learning much more than content in school. They are learning how to leverage content to make society better.

It is not the technology that will make the difference in pace or choice for Joe's students. However, technology certainly has the potential to accelerate personalized learning. Technology is used because it is beneficial to the student, not because it is the hot trend. Technology allows teachers and students to access specialized materials well beyond textbooks, in multiple formats, with few constraints on time or space. It offers innovative platforms for collaboration in knowledge creation, where teachers can share and enrich teaching materials. Perhaps most importantly, technology can support new pedagogies that focus on learners as active participants with tools for inquiry-based pedagogies and collaborative workspaces. Technology can enhance experiential learning, foster project-based and inquiry-based pedagogies, facilitate hands-on activities and co-operative learning, and deliver formative real-time assessments. It can also support learning and teaching communities with new tools, such as remote and virtual labs, interactive, non-linear courseware based on state-of-the-art instructional design, sophisticated software for experimentation and simulation, social media and serious games.

We have a choice to make. We can choose the easy path of using technology to personalize content without regard to the more important skills and competencies our children will need to be successful in their future, or we can choose to fulfill our moral obligation to the next generation to fully prepare them to be successful in the complex world into which we are sending them. As Koen Timmers will show in the next chapter, technology must be used properly if it is to effectively prepare our pupils for life beyond school. It must, as he argues, be directed towards each student's background, interests and passions. History will show effective personalization in education optimized by great teachers to be a critical goal as we approach 2030.

Chapter 7

Evolution of Technology in the Classroom

Koen Timmers

Six years ago, a student of mine had a habit of fact-checking me on Twitter while I taught. At times he would confront me, claiming Twitter "experts" were disproving my facts. As you can imagine, I didn't enjoy these interactions. My first reaction was to close down all social media for students on our school campus.

I was wrong.

Since then, I have embraced social media and have discovered its fantastic power in education. Social media is just one example of how technology has entered the classroom and changed learning practices. Its impact ranges from digitizing textbooks, providing equity in education through assistive technology and reaching isolated students, to allowing global collaborations to solve real problems important to students.

As we sail through the 21st century, technology in the classroom is becoming more and more predominant. Tablets, social media, electronic learning platforms, 3D printers, games and other technologies are finding their way to classrooms. The Fourth Industrial Revolution will only further exacerbate technology's influence. Students need to know how to use technology to not only learn, but to also use technology to apply their knowledge to real situations. Teachers need to find effective ways to incorporate it in ways that boost understanding and provide avenues for making learning relevant.

While I was studying to become a teacher, I was introduced to the wonders of the Internet for the first time. Instantly, I was drawn to its power to connect me to other people and easily access information. My love of computer science started with the development of my own webpages in the nascent stages of the World Wide Web. Teaching computer science early in my career involved technology that would seem obsolete to my students today: overhead projectors, poorly copied paper learning materials and monochrome monitors. Now, the online school I established has over 20,000 students who access 60 digital courses. All learning materials are instantly accessible from anywhere in the world at any time of day. Students can communicate with the author of their digital textbook and get feedback on their work from peers and teachers instantly. This shift has happened in less than 20 years. With the rate of innovation increasing exponentially in the Fourth Industrial Revolution, we must prepare our students and our teachers for even greater changes that will happen in much shorter timeframes.

Technology is a pedagogical catalyst. It can make good classroom practices great, and it can make bad classroom practices even worse. If we are to prepare our students to meet the challenges of their future in a rapidly changing world, teachers must be prepared to use technology well. Never has the danger of poor pedagogy been more pronounced or the benefits of digitally aided good practice been greater. Educational technology can be of huge benefit to children if it is used correctly with a focus on the intricacies of student age, content area, financial resources of the school, policy, culture and religious makeup of the community.

The Evolution of Learning with Technology

Technology has always been a disruptive force in education. At one time, the slate, the ballpoint pen and the slide rule were all considered new "educational technology," and debates raged on whether to ban them from classrooms. From the time of Socrates, when he worried that the written word would have a negative effect on his pupils' memory, there has been resistance in education to new innovations.[1] Now, in a time of exponential growth in technological innovation, the relevance of an education system will be defined by its ability to reflect the digital reality outside of the classroom. If videoconferencing across distances and cultures is commonplace in the workplace, schools must give students experience in this practice. If resources in the workplace are updated in real time as new information becomes available, educational resources must be as well.

---

1 How Much of Your Life You're Wasting on You Commute. *Washington Post*. Retrieved from www.washingtonpost.com/news/wonk/wp/2016/02/25/how-much-of-your-life-youre-wasting-on-your-commute

Textbooks and standardized learning materials have long been central to the learning that happens in classrooms. Before the Internet made information quick and easy to obtain, textbooks were vital sources of information in schools. Standardization of knowledge and learning worked well for education prior to the Internet age, but its limitations became more apparent in the 21st century. Teachers who only follow scripted textbook lessons cannot foster the critical thinking, collaboration, communication skills and creativity required for success in today's world. The Fourth Industrial Revolution will continue to increase the democratization of information and will demand even more innovation, abstract thinking and emotional intelligence. Standardization will be ever more obsolete.

Simply utilizing digital resources will not improve student outcomes, nor will it prepare our next generation for the realities of their future after graduation. OECD's 2015 report on students, computers and learning showed that well-implemented technology combined with excellent teaching practices can have great positive impact on student outcomes, but increased computer usage in schools had a negative correlation with student reading scores.[2] Schools and teachers are not using technology effectively at a time when doing so is more important than ever.

The Future of Skills Study done by Pearson, Nesta and the Oxford Martin School found that balancing uniquely human skills with technology will chart the course of our workforce in the future. Education systems will have to support and spread teaching practices that best facilitate this. The study finds that the education of teachers on these practices, both before entering the profession and while they are in service, will be of paramount importance.[3]

Digital Textbooks

I teach web design, a subject which changes very fast, faster than the refresh cycle of textbooks. Since 2000, I have been writing my own textbooks to provide students with a quality up-to-date and relevant resource. In certain subjects, there's a distinction between what is presented in a textbook and what's taught by the teacher. Teachers may mention facts which aren't in the textbook, the sequence may be

2 www.oecd.org/publications/students-computers-and-learning-9789264239555-en.htm
3 http://futureskills.pearson.com

different or some chapters may be skipped entirely. In addition to the digital textbook, I began to create documents for each lesson, saved on the school's intranet, so that students were able to rehearse at home. This presented two issues:

- Students who were absent, had to wait until I came to school to receive their requested documents because I could not share outside of the local intranet.
- At the end of a semester, it wasn't that easy to find information in the multitude of separate documents.

I decided to create my digital textbook using MS OneNote™ to solve these two issues. It has the ability to combine multiple forms of media, its organizational features, sharing and search options. The tool uses sections and pages that greatly improves the organization of a whole semester of work. Teachers can provide a rich multimedia experience by easily recording audio, adding multimedia and 3D artifacts from a variety of sources. The search function searches through text, handwriting, images and audio. Furthermore, the sharing features allow students to access the content anywhere, anytime on any device, even outside the school's intranet. While these features are wonderfully convenient, more importantly, my textbooks were 100 per cent up to date and to the point. Students were able to maximize their time on task and solving problems because they received what they needed, at the level required without wasting time on irrelevant content. Good teachers are best suited to judge which parts of textbooks are relevant, outdated or needed to offer their students the most effective learning experience.

I began to strive for a paperless classroom. Once students get used to a new workflow, most preferred the digital format. Only a minority of students requested a printout. Since my students were able to edit my document, they even began to correct my typos. The ability for students to edit can go terribly wrong if they were to delete sections on purpose. Luckily, OneNote and most cloud solutions offers version control to go back in time and restore previous, intact versions.

Around the globe, teachers are finding that the resources they have traditionally used are becoming obsolete as new innovations find their way into the learning environment. By using the digital pen and projector screen in my classroom, I was able to replace my chalkboard with enhanced presentation strategies. I was able to rescale and annotate on top of quality pictures. The resources could be easily shared with parallel classrooms and even saved for future years.

Digital assistive tools are now offering amazing opportunities to students, especially those with disabilities. Previous generations of students had limited resources adapted to their individual needs. Camera apps can convert paper documents and images to digital text almost instantly and for no additional cost; this process previously took months and at great expense. Digitizing documents makes studying easier for students who find organizing papers difficult or for those who would like to study in places where papers are hard to manage. Learning tools help dyslexic students improve their reading, writing and spelling.[4] Text-to-speech and speech-to-text software is becoming better and more widely used to help children overcome issues with eyesight and fine motor coordination. Assistive technologies will become increasingly available, significantly closing the equity gap in education.

Phalla Neang has been a teacher, school director and countrywide coordinator for the Education for Blind program in Cambodia. Perceptions of those who are blind in her country are often extremely negative, with many citizens believing the disability was caused by misbehavior in past lives. There is widespread belief that blind children were incapable of learning. Phalla was determined to change those perceptions and find ways to help her students.

Screen-reading software and other technologies were vital to her efforts. Phalla used a combination of new digital tools and a program focused in modalities that are more natural to those who are blind, such as music, touch and foreign languages in order to prepare her students for a global world. Her program was so successful that 100 per cent of her visually impaired secondary students passed the national examination of baccalaureate. Perceptions of the abilities of blind students are changing in Cambodia, and Phalla's methodologies have spread to 69 teachers in schools around the country.

Connecting to their Learning by Connecting to the World

As a student, I learned about several topics using boring textbooks. I now realize that I remember very little of these topics because there was no emotional connection to the topic and thus a lack of engagement. The more students experience learning connections to situations

---

4 https://news.microsoft.com/en-gb/2017/02/10/dyslexic-children-perform-positively-reading-tests-using-onenote/

outside the classroom, the more emotionally connected to the content they become. Michael Soskil, 2016 Global Teacher Prize finalist and Pennsylvania Teacher of the Year 2017, advocates: "Students need global learning experiences. It's hard to change the world when you don't know much about it." Mareike Hachemer, another Global Teacher Prize finalist, agrees and tries to infuse global competencies into her curriculum. She states "for cultural understanding, connections to real people are crucial and so I decided to offer students around the world experiences that broadened their worldview. They were able to learn by connecting with peers around the word."

During the past year, I set up three global educational projects, the Wai Water, the Human Differences[5] and the Climate Action Projects. Each of them were connected to several United Nations Sustainable Development Goals (SDGs). I managed to use social media and other technologies to connect thousands of children and schools across six continents.

The projects provide opportunities for teachers to personalize learning practices that meet the needs of students, while still allowing them to focus on issues that affect all of us on this planet. Each student can see a role they can play, and it is contextualized for their particular situation. What's better than learning about global issues directly from students living in those countries? The digital tools allowed students to learn from each other, something prohibitively slow or expensive for previous generations. Students built the empathy that is necessary for the future health of our globally connected society.

The projects were student centered. The teachers weren't allowed to give away knowledge. They had to guide the discussions and make sure that their students verified their resources. The project covered several subjects like math, science, biology, literature etc. Rather than learning about water or geography or climate change via textbooks, students used 5 weeks to learn in stages: by exploring, discussing, brainstorming, presenting the findings in their own classroom, and by watching videos from their peers across the world. Finally, they connected via Skype during the projects last week.

Creativity is triggered, and students become invested when they become knowledge builders. In the Human Differences project,[6] students had to focus on gender equality as well as address the question of

5 The Human Differences Project. Retrieved from www.humandifferences.com
6 Climate Action Project. Retrieved from www.climate-action.info

why countries decide to build walls – a subject which has been relevant for many centuries. Rather than memorizing facts via textbooks, students used Lego to express their feelings, created stop-motion videos using green screens, went on excursions and invited their parents to the classroom.

The Nigerian students composed their own song. The Tunisian students developed a computer game. The Argentinian students used Minecraft to present their findings about walls. The Swedish students created an equality machine, which is now exhibited in the city library. The Egyptian students even came to school for 5 weeks during summer vacation. Students are engaged because the technologies allowed students to express their opinions and gave validity to their collective voice. The technology allowed them to open a two-way dialogue.

The Climate Action project involved 250 schools over 69 countries and was supported by His Holiness the Dalai Lama, the Jane Goodall foundation, Greenpeace, United Nations Educational, Scientific and Cultural Organization, WWF and many more public figures. Experts like Celiné Cousteau, Richard E. Hyman and Dr. Languell shared their stories and passion about climate change. Michael Dunlea stated: "I seriously think this was the best day of my teaching career What an incredible experience."

Technology was instrumental in making these projects such a success.

• Students were able to see how topical the projects were to either them or to their new global friends connected by technology. For instance, Irish students had to close their schools for the very first time due to a hurricane. It offered the right angle to introduce the Climate Action project. During the project, students' perspectives were changed because of the Flooding in Sierra Leone and South Africa.

• Students made deeper connections to the subject and were triggered to find solutions. In the Climate Action project, Nigerian students developed their own small biogas plant. Global Teacher Prize finalist Joe Fatheree took the lead in a challenge in which students over 50 countries created an eco-friendly world in Minecraft. Canadian students explored the potential of using mealworms to biodegrading Styrofoam and other plastics and 3D printed coral reef to create artificial reefs in hopes of slowing down coral bleaching in the world's oceans.

The combination of broad questions, with teachers guiding at the side and many kinds of technologies, allowed all students to be creative and express themselves. They had to learn to communicate and collaborate with peers. A few students claimed that they noticed for the very first time their opinion mattered. US teacher Kylee Babish witnessed:

> They are demonstrating progress towards and mastery of learning standards through their voice and choice, engaging with credible content and expressing their learning. Students are individually and collaboratively contributing to the organization, research, written and spoken scripts, filming, and presenting on the overall project each week. Finally, they are providing feedback to each other, themselves, and absolutely love to look at the other countries' projects.

In this case students, technology and the collaborative learning approach made a successful combination, since students were engaged and were able to practice skills other than recall. Most of them had indelible experiences that will persist for 5, 10 or even 20 years.

When we say "global citizenship education," we're talking about teaching students to communicate, collaborate, think critically and creatively, with the ultimate goal of taking action to improve conditions both locally and globally. According to employers, new employees are missing those very skills.[7] Organizations outside education are now looking at ways to provide opportunity for students to develop empathy and global citizenship.

* Empatico is an initiative of the KIND Foundation that is endeavoring to connect students in classrooms around the world using videoconferencing technology and activities that help children learn empathy. The KIND Foundation was created to foster communities that are healthier, more empathetic, and embrace their shared humanity. They explain: "As students learn together, they explore their similarities and differences with curiosity and kindness and develop practical communication and leadership skills."[8]

---

7 Educators don't have to choose between educating for global citizenship and educating for a better economy: https://blog.educationandskillsforum.org/educators-dont-have-to-choose-between-educating-for-the-global-economy-or-for-global-citizenship/?utm_content=buffer7163a&utm_medium=social&utm_source=facebook.com&utm_campaign=buffer
8 https://empatico.org/team

- Microsoft's Skype in the Classroom website is an online community that enables teachers from around the world opportunity to "inspire the next generation of global citizens through transformative learning over Skype."[9] Through collaborative lessons, games that allow children from different cultures to play together, virtual field trips and virtual guest speakers, the platform helps educators leverage videoconferencing to give children a global perspective.

In recent years, technology has made it relatively inexpensive and time effective to reach out into the world. The speed and reach of technology are unprecedented and fairly ubiquitous opening so many more ways to contextualize and personalize student learning, going well beyond facts.

Equity by Distance Education

Education is a human right. Everyone, everywhere has a need and the right to quality education. Never has that been more apparent to me than the time in 2015 as I stared across a computer screen at teachers at the Kakuma Refugee Camp in northwestern Kenya. They have almost nothing, but parents in the camp yearn for their children to receive an education that will lead to a better life. I saw this in their eyes, heard it in their words, and felt it in my soul as we spoke.

Emotional experiences inspire action. I realized that the same technology that was giving me a window into the camp and allowing me to learn of the problems in Kakuma, could be used to provide education in a place that lacked qualified teachers, learning materials and basic resources. I began to provide lessons for students and professional training for teachers via Skype. To help with their lack of current technology, I even sent my personal laptop to the camp. FlimAid, a non-governmental organization working in the camp, committed to providing Internet access and electricity to make the project successful. Immediately, the refugees were excited about the new opportunity available to them, and eventually demanded more connections than I could handle on my own. I created a global network of educators who voluntarily taught Kakuma refugees through Skype. It wasn't long before that network swelled to over one hundred educators from 40 different countries.

---

9 https://education.microsoft.com/skype-in-the-classroom/overview

The Kakuma project[10] is just one example of how anytime, anywhere ed-tech can close the gap in education for isolated populations. There are many other ways where previously isolated students can be connected. Much to the dismay of students in wintery climates who look forward to school cancellations due to snow, digital solutions are now available that allow students to continue their school day when previously poor weather would have made it impossible.[11]

CVO De Verdieping decided in 2007 to implement distance learning in the web design department. They chose to offer remote synchronous learning via a web conferencing tool for half of the classes. A teacher teaching live and virtually is able to maintain the teacher–student relationship, which is much more challenging than just providing a pre-recorded lecture.

Teaching virtually means that one could conceivably teach from anywhere. Teaching at home may drive educators outside their comfort zone as it initially gives the impression they are talking to their laptop screen. Schools need to provide training to both teachers and student. The atmosphere of virtual live teaching may approach the atmosphere of face-to-face learning once teachers and students are accustomed to this strategy and are confronted with the benefits of remote learning. Distance learning has distinct benefits and disadvantages.

In a technical context, access to devices and connectivity must be considered. Schools need to offer an alternative to students who don't have access to computer or Internet connection. They may dedicate one classroom to the distance learning project and offer free devices to be borrowed by students. There are new solutions being deployed that will significantly reduce the question of ubiquitous connectivity. Hurricane Maria destroyed all of the towers that provided cell and mobile data services on the island of Puerto Rico. Alphabet Inc. used solar-powered stratospheric balloons to solve this problem. Project Loon allowed citizens of the island to text, email, and have basic Internet access.[12] The company has been developing this technology as a means to develop a "sustainable internet ecosystem" in Africa.[13] It is likely

---

10 www.projectkakuma.com
11 www.cnn.com/2014/02/23/living/snow-days-virtual-schools/index.html
12 www.latimes.com/business/technology/la-fi-tn-puerto-rico-balloons-20171021-story.
html
13 www.dw.com/en/googles-plans-to-expand-internet-access-in-africa-is-about-the-data/a-16903897

that other cost-effective solutions to the connectivity problem will be developed.

Pedagogically speaking, there may be some differences between students learning computer science at a local school and at home. At school, students might view a classroom display in addition to their own screen for their own work. Some students working from home decide to use two computer screens or a second device so they can follow the lesson on one screen and maintain a screen for their personal work. Most web conferencing tools allow teachers to record sessions, which provides unprecedented benefits to students who want to review. This is particularly beneficial for students who miss school or who are studying in a second language. Since much of a class is students working, the screencasts of the lecture can get to the point with a maximum 10-minute video.

Distance learning is eco-friendly, avoiding the financial and environmental costs of a daily commute. However, some students are very keen on the social contact in face-to-face settings, and it's very hard for teachers to read their students' emotions, which is an important part of education. Asynchronous virtual teaching further distances the student from the teacher. There is a lower chance of success in programs that are 100 per cent distance learning combined with the choice of pace self-paced and the autonomy of self directed learning.[14] The ability to enroll at all times makes it harder for teachers to offer synchronous learning via web conferencing tools. While this may be attractive for people who combine work with studies, only half of the students do complete their course. Armand elaborates on why this personalization model doesn't work in Chapter 6. Putting students in contact with each other may combat this low rate of success.

Collaboration

The need for students to develop the capacity to communicate with each other and collaborate across cultural and geographic boundaries has never been greater. According to a World Economic Forum white paper on Realizing Human Potential in the Fourth Industrial Revolution, "technology is rapidly altering the ways we interact and work, linking communities and workers in increasingly sophisticated ways and opening up new opportunities."[15] In their Future of Jobs report,

14 Park, J. H. (2007). *Factors Related to Learner Dropout in Online Learning.* USA: ERIC.
15 www3.weforum.org/docs/WEF_EGW_Whitepaper.pdf

people management, coordinating with others, emotional intelligence and negotiation are all listed among the ten most important skills in the 2020 workforce.[16] As the world continues to become more globalized and interconnected, the ability to understand diverse perspectives and work with those that have divergent worldviews will become increasingly important. Machines and computers will be collaborating in unprecedented ways in the near future.[17] We must ensure our students are developing the skills necessary to collaborate within human networks.

Students need good skills which prepare them for a future job. In many schools, students are currently mainly being assessed on lower-level thinking skills such as memorization and recall. Future employers will need to quickly adapt to a culture of collaboration. They will need to collaborate with others within and outside of the organization, often using a number of new technologies.

In addition to needing practice at collaborating as a competency in and of itself, collaborative learning is considered one of the most effective ways to improve learning.[18] Berge[19] advocates that learning requires two main types of interaction: interaction with the course content and interaction with other people. Anderson et al.[20] argue that there is evidence that providing opportunities for meaningful interaction with other students and community members in the context of structured learning activities enhances learning.

Vygotsky[21] suggests that social constructivism is at the heart of why collaboration is such an effective learning strategy. Constructivism is more than putting students into a group and throwing them a question. Students learn by exploring, connecting, discussing, creating and evaluating in a network. They learn from nodes which can be peers, teachers, books, websites, blogs and social media. The teacher becomes a discussion

16 www.weforum.org/agenda/2016/01/the-10-skills-you-need-to-thrive-in-the-fourth-industrial-revolution/

17 www.digitalistmag.com/digital-economy/2016/04/26/collaborative-networks-forefront-of-fourth-industrial-revolution-04169100

18 Jef Staes. Retrieved from www.jefstaes.com/prepare

19 Berge, Z. L. (2002). Active, Interactive, and Reflective E-Learning. *Quarterly Review of Distance Education*, 3: 181–90.

20 Anderson, T. & Dron, J. (2014). *Teaching Crowds: Learning and Social Media*. Unpublished, 101.

21 Vygotsky, L. S. (1978). *Mind and Society: The Development of Higher Mental Processes*. Cambridge, MA: Harvard University Press.

leader, pointing the students in the right direction. While constructivism doesn't necessarily have to be connected to ICT, forums, email and web conferencing can expand our initial notions of small group discussions. A Massive Open Online Course (MOOC) has open access via the web with unlimited attendance;[22] this can provide a large network for collaboration. Personal learning networks (PLN) are informal learning networks in which a person makes a connection with another person with the specific intent that some type of learning will occur because of that connection.[23]

In my classroom, an incredible phenomenon started to occur when students were given increased autonomy over editable digital content. Children felt empowered enough to begin correcting the textbook that I had created for them. They collectively, not just me their teacher, owned the learning in the classroom. Of course, I encouraged them to expand their learning by adding their own pages of new learning to the textbook. Students spontaneously began to create and share own written tutorials which brought us to a very interesting new scenario: students began to learn from each other. I began to learn from my students and share their work with other classes. The fluidity of the digital world makes this type of process reasonable.

Teachers are still having difficult times with students knowing more about certain topics than they do. They struggle with the perception from parents that "I hope my child has a good teacher" equates with the teacher being the master of all knowledge lecturing in the front of the classroom. I believe teachers need to cope with this taboo and need to strive for a situation in which students aren't limited to the teacher's knowledge. I met American teachers who have surrendered to the idea that students will know more than the teacher and have taught coding to 13-year-olds, without knowing how to code themselves. The flipped learning model provides many avenues to learning without going through the teacher at the front of the class.

As digital tools such as YouTube and mobile phones have allowed easy digital recording and playback of video, "flipping" students have the ability to consume content outside the classroom. Videos can be created by teachers for students, by students for their peers, or accessed from online sources such as Khan Academy to supplement their in-school learning. Benefits of flipping include being able to watch at convenient times, the

22 Anderson, T. & Dron, J. (2014). *Teaching Crowds: Learning and Social Media*. Unpublished, 101.
23 Vygotsky, L. S. (1978). *Mind and Society: The Development of Higher Mental Processes*. Cambridge, MA: Harvard University Press.

ability to rewind and playback information, and the ability for teachers to create increased time for face-to-face interactions during the school day. By creating instructional videos, teachers can make their curriculum partly flexible and differentiate their classroom. Teachers do not necessarily need to be flip learning during all classes. The key to flip learning is to use class time to get students to create and showcase understanding of the content. They get the opportunity to work with the content.

Sometimes, the advantages to using ed-tech are obvious and sometimes there are unintended consequences. I asked students to drop their questions in the chat window so as not to interrupt the virtual class. My intent was to follow up at the end of the session. I soon discovered that the students began to solve each other's questions. This was especially true of shy students. In most cases they absolutely love to be involved, contrasting greatly with the face-to-face settings in which they are too shy to participate. When combining remote and face-to-face classes, the shy students become more involved during face-to-face classes as well. Normal schools are well suited for extroverts, but introverts often find it difficult to navigate a social space where there is little opportunity to find quiet time to process information. In most school cultures where being social and outgoing are prized above all else, it can be difficult, even shameful, to be an introvert. But, as Susan Cain argues "introverts bring extraordinary talents and abilities to the world, and should be encouraged and celebrated."[24]

Used properly as student-centered tools, ed-tech can allow social constructivism through collaboration to change the depth of learning between students who were previously disconnected by distance, by access to teachers, by access to quality peers, or by the social biases of a face-to-face classroom.

The Rise of Social Media

Social media makes quite an impact on our daily life. Twitter breaks the news, like the occasion when US Airways flight ditched in New York's Hudson river.[25] Facebook played a significant role during the Arab spring.[26] Nonprofits used social media to mobilize rescue efforts after

---

24 The Power of Introverts, Susan Cain. Retrieved from www.ted.com/talks/susan_cain_the_power_of_introverts#t-3436
25 New York Plane Crash Twitter Breaks the News Again. *The Telegraph*. Retrieved from www.telegraph.co.uk/technology/twitter/4269765/New-York-plane-crash-Twitter-breaks-the-news-again.html
26 Social Media and the Arab Spring. *Wikipedia*. Retrieved from https://en.wikipedia.org/wiki/Social_media_and_the_Arab_Spring

the earthquake in Haiti.[27] Social media has affected the lives of journalists, artists and even presidents. Many people are using social media. According to usage statistics gathered earlier this year by Ofcom, 66 per cent of all adults aged 16+ have a profile on at least one social networking site.[28] While some schools ban social media, others see educational opportunities. Can social media stimulate our students' learning processes?

There is a distinction between open and closed social media. We can't compare closed Facebook groups to an open Twitter timeline. In educational settings, a small network may be sufficient to discuss, brainstorm, explore, offer feedback and share within a classroom.

Not only do schools have a duty to teach students how to use social media, but these networks can also support all kinds of learning. Students can connect to experts, peers, parents and teachers on Twitter or LinkedIn. I organized a closed Facebook group which allowed my students to post questions, to inform each other, post extra resources etc. In most cases, the questions were already answered before I even was able to read them. The interesting part is that students over different classrooms are able to exchange thoughts and even students who were graduated remain in the group and are able to offer specialized feedback based on their experience in the work field. Students can learn by watching videos on YouTube or creating content to be published on Tumblr or YouTube. They can collaborate in wikis, can reflect on blogs and offer formative feedback by commenting on their peers' posts. Hashtags for individual courses allow students to access the discussion easily. Early data from some of the most successful MOOCs indicates that student participation is greatly increased when social media platforms are integrated with the learning program.[29] Students have to learn to network to find and share information.

Social media triggers a dopamine high. It affects the brain in the same way that a hug does.[30] Every week during the Wai Water, the Human Differences and the Climate Action Projects, the submissions

27 Social Lessons from the Haiti Earthquake Relief Effort. *Mashable*. Retrieved from http://mashable.com/2010/01/20/social-media-lessons-haiti
28 Adults Media Use and Attitudes. *Ofcom*. Retrieved from www.ofcom.org.uk/__data/assets/pdf_file/0026/80828/2016-adults-media-use-and-attitudes.pdf
29 How Social Media Is Changing Education. *BBC Active*. Retrieved from www.bbcactive.com/BBCActiveIdeasandResources/Howsocialmediaischangingeducation.aspx
30 Social Media Triggers a Dopamine High. Retrieved from www.ama.org/publications/MarketingNews/Pages/feeding-the-addiction.aspx

and actions of those who got great feedback and likes, became stronger since they felt empowered, liked and supported. But those students who did not get much feedback, did not improve much and in many cases, didn't complete the project. This demonstrates the importance of ensuring teachers, parents and community members provide feedback to their students.

Social media comes with some serious drawbacks, such as privacy issues and the potential to spread fake news. Our digital footprint is getting larger and with facial recognition, tracking cookies and personalized marketing, it will become very hard to save your privacy. Students need to learn not to share too much personal data or build relationships with people whom you cannot trust. We need to inform our kids how they can defend themselves, while we still teach them to network. Students may be confronted with inappropriate content and comments. Fake news has always existed; it was commonly known as gossip or misinformation. It becomes increasingly important for social media users to be able to identify bias in all sources and be able to get facts and real information.[31] Since most of the students will face these same issues in their regular lives, I believe it is the school's duty to prepare for this new reality of connected life. This chapter opened with a story of one of my students using Twitter experts to contradict my lesson. I was wrong to ask them not to use Twitter while I was teaching. Instead I should have pointed out that not every self-proclaimed expert is right and then connected them with peers around the world to broaden their view of life.

Don't take social media too much for granted though. In the Fourth Industrial Revolution, technology can be replaced very fast. World leading companies may be replaced by new alternatives. During the past year Twitter has had to close their offices in Germany, Belgium and the Netherlands. If Facebook is obsolete by 2030, it will certainly be replaced by something even more powerful.

Today, technology can provide an unprecedented education, by closing the gap to populations by geography, socio-economics, weather or learning disabilities. Students can leverage social constructivism as they discover the role that they can play in solving global problems, while simultaneously making connections to new global friends free of alternative facts and propaganda.

31 Building a Global Debunker for Fake News. *World Economic Forum*. Retrieved from www.weforum.org/agenda/2017/05/global-debunker-fake-news/

There is much about our future that is unknown, but we can be sure that technological innovation will continue to impact education. Decisions will have to be made in every level of our educational systems to ensure that impact is positive. Countries will have to decide how to allocate resources, schools will have to determine strategies to meet the needs of their communities, and teachers will continually be forced to determine how best to serve their students. Those decisions must be driven by compassion, student need, and skill development rather than being solely based on content delivery and convenience.

There are no simple, easy answers to the complex questions we will face about how to prepare our children for the unpredictable world into which they will graduate, and technology will never be a panacea. For example, in our rush to digitize learning, we might be too quick to trade handwriting for typing. We must be cognizant that students might need to be able to write by hand because Mueller and Oppenheimer[32] claim that handwriting is key to learning because it is slower than typing and by slowing down the process of taking notes, you accelerate learning. We must be thoughtful and perhaps skeptically optimistic as we allow technology to evolve in the classroom.

Vikas Potas, CEO Varkey Foundation, argues:

> Politicians across the spectrum are united in proclaiming that education is the answer to automation, skills training, and retraining for those whose jobs that will disappear. But new data suggests that we simply don't have enough teachers to teach these new skills that the country will need.[33]

All the international evidence – from Finland to South Korea – shows that it is impossible to create an excellent education system without well-motivated, well-trained and fairly rewarded teachers.

The preparation of our teachers needs to focus on giving them the same innovative mindset, adaptability and critical thinking that we hope to instill in our students. In the sectors outside of education, employee training is often among the largest budget line items

---

32 Berge, Z. L. (2002). Active, Interactive, and Reflective E-Learning. *Quarterly Review of Distance Education*, 3: 181–90.

33 The 'March of the Machines' and the Teacher Recruitment Crisis together Make for a Disastrous Cocktail. *TES*. Retrieved from www.tes.com/news/school-news/breaking-views/march-machines-and-teacher-recruitment-crisis-together-make-a

for organizations.[34] Inside education, OECD's 2015 TALIS (Teaching and Learning International Survey) report found that almost half of teachers reported not having participated in any professional development activities related to ICT in the last year.[35] That report concludes, "it is teachers' professional development, as well as their beliefs about work, that are key to unlocking technology's potential for teaching and learning." To prepare our next generation to succeed in the Fourth Industrial Revolution, a more targeted focus on professional education of teachers, along with significant investment in these efforts will be necessary. Professional development done on the cheap will almost certainly have little impact.[36]

Given the expected shortage of well-trained teachers, the quest for standardization and the advancements in Artificial Intelligence, it is not difficult to imagine the desire to offload much of the work of a teacher to an automated computer system. This is a slippery slope. A teacher must use professional judgement to match the best pedagogical tool to the unique situation in the learning environment. Skilled teachers make these determinations in ways that robots and computer algorithms cannot. No standardized textbook program, algorithm or computer program will be able to meet student needs in these situations as well as a compassionate and well-educated teacher. This aspect of a teacher's practice is why professional education and professional autonomy are critical. And, as Jelmer Evers will argue in the next chapter, it is incumbent on each teacher to take responsibility for their own autonomy and rediscover the purpose of education. As trusted individuals, they should seek to use technology wisely, as a catalyst for great learning, a more equitable world and indeed world peace.

34 www.litmos.com/wp-content/uploads/2016/12/BHG-training-budget-benchmarks-report-2017.pdf
35 www.keepeek.com/Digital-Asset-Management/oecd/education/teaching-with-technology_5jrxnhpp6p8v-en#.Wft-QhNSz6Z#page3
36 https://ideas.repec.org/p/nbr/nberwo/8916.html

Chapter 8

Flip the System

The Networked Activist Teacher

Jelmer Evers

"So Jelmer, are we going to have World War III?" Quite an entry, right? But that was the start of my school year. A smaller class of pre-university students. They were mostly girls and very socially conscious. They were looking at me expectantly. This was the very first history lesson of the year, and the first time that I taught them. I wanted to start the school year by going over what they wanted to learn, what was in the curriculum – 20th Century World History – and what I thought was important and might be interesting. I think students need to be invested in what they learn, and it is always surprising and insightful what they know and are interested in learning about. And they came up with a broad range of topics: Black Lives Matter and how that related to slavery and segregation in the United States. Inequality and the rise of populism. Fascism and National Socialism. One thing stood out. They were definitely interested in the Interbellum. "Do you think that is what is happening now, Jelmer"? And then the step to World War III is not that far away. I get the World War III question once every so often. In the years after 9/11, it was more prevalent. After the Great Recession of 2008 as well. But during those years, I could quite confidently say no. But this time, it felt different. When I explained why, I think they felt my unease as well. It was one of those profound moments that every teacher recognizes.

"May you live in interesting times," as the saying goes.[1] A cliché maybe, but true nonetheless. Maybe this is accurate for every age. But the present feels more urgent than it did when I started teaching in 2003. That is why I struggled with the question. It seems that history is back with a vengeance and the political, social and economic fault

---

1 It is not a Chinese saying and the origins are quite unclear. Probably American. https://quoteinvestigator.com/2015/12/18/live/

lines that are appearing nationally and internationally make the question about how we build the systems to ensure a quality education for all, all the more urgent. I completely agree with both Klaus Schwab and Dennis Shirley that there is an urgency, but also a promise of the present moment. Crises also enable us to make new connections and build new institutions that allow us to create a better future.[2]

After the lesson I was very quiet as I pondered how lucky I am that I have the freedom to design my lessons like this, that I have the freedom to seize moments like this and take responsibility for the present and my students. This is what students need, but this is not what far too many students get. The question is how do we get there?

Woke

It was a personal crisis of my professional identity as a teacher 8 years earlier that started my work on helping to develop an empowered Dutch teaching profession. The Dutch educational system increasingly left me feeling disempowered, estranged and boxed in as a teacher, expecting actions and judgements from me that weren't good for my students, my colleagues and the Dutch education system as a whole. This was until I arrived at my new school, UniC. Teaching there was a life-changing experience for me. UniC is a secondary school with a very progressive vision and design. What I found were students who were responsible, curious and empathic. Colleagues who were reflective and constantly asking themselves: Why are we doing this? My practice changed completely: working collaboratively, co-teaching and working across subject on project-based learning. But also, still teaching traditionally – I love talking about history. It was the best of both worlds. What arguably influenced me the most was probably the work of Max van Manen on what he calls pedagogical tact. The emphasis on the relational and caring aspect of our profession "teaching require tact – an interpretive intelligence, a practical moral intuitiveness, a sensitivity and openness toward the child's subjectivity, and an improvisational resoluteness in dealing with children."[3]

There were three particular things that set me off on a more political path. The first thing was a visit by the Dutch inspectorate to my

2 Shirley, D. (2016). *The New Imperatives of Educational Change*. New York: Routledge.
3 Van Manen, M. (1991). *The Tact of Teaching: The Meaning of Pedagogical Thoughtfulness*. Albany: State University of New York Press.

school. The school was under improvement measures because of failing exam scores. We acknowledged this and were confident that our improvement efforts would soon pay off (they did), whilst keeping our vision intact (partly). The inspectorate praised our pedagogical climate, but in the end, it was only hard numbers that counted, and we were strongly advised to change our practices, meaning conform to the standard. These conclusions were being made on the basis of half-a-day 20-minute lesson observations in the school. I had finally found a school where students and teachers could flourish, and found that the system didn't allow for that deviation from the standard. I was furious. And I was "woke" as they call it today. I was already successfully blogging about pedagogy and educational technology, but from then on, my blogging became more political. The second thing was a particular conversation on educational change with one of my students, Tycho. He asked me: "If you're so passionate about this, why don't you do something about it?" I really didn't know, but the thought has never left me again.

The third one was a statement by our new state secretary of education. A Dutch politician from the same political party had just described us teachers as living in the stone age, and the state secretary was calling for more standardized testing, rankings and performance pay. I was livid by so much ignorance from politicians and said so on Twitter. Another more traditional teacher and prominent writer, Rene Kneyber, was furious as well, and although we had never met, we decided then and there to write an opinion piece that evening collaboratively online. The article was published in a major national newspaper in which we disputed all these points raised by the state secretary.[4] To his credit the secretary invited us immediately for a conversation. This episode became the basis for our books and ideas in *Het Alternatief (The Alternative): weg met de afrekencultuur in het onderwijs* and *Flip the System: changing education from the ground up*.[5]

I had become an activist teacher and came to the realization that every teacher should be one. Writing *Het Alternatief* and *Flip the System* made me realize how connected global issues and international

4 Evers, J. & Kneyber, R. (2012). Het onderwijs wordt niet beter van al die ranglijsten. *NRC Handelsblad.*

5 Evers, J. & Kneyber, R. (2013). *Het alternatief: weg met de afrekencultuur in het onderwijs!* Amsterdam: Boom. and Evers, J. & Kneyber, R. (2015). *Flip the System: Changing Education from the Ground Up.* Abingdon, UK: Routledge.

education policy are to our ability to teach in what we collectively deem to be good. At a minimum, we need to be aware as teachers how global forces influence our classrooms. But the real solution lies in being an activist part of that global community and advocate for our students, and ourselves.[6]

Political Decay

Others have already explored the impact of the Fourth Industrial Revolution on different levels in this book, and I'd like stress two particular points here: the political aspect and the need for strong public institutions. Margaret Thatcher captured so much of what went wrong in the last 40 years in one sentence when she infamously said: "There is no such thing as society."[6]

The decline of our post-war political order is closely linked to rising inequality. Thomas Piketty's work *Capital in the 21st Century* was a milestone in this regard.[7] Many works have been published recently that support his findings and have provided empirical data for the case that inequality is rising and there are severe political long-term effects. The general consensus–in stark contrast to the 1980s, 1990s and 2000s – is that unbridled capitalism – allowing market forces to permeate through every part of society – will lead to a rent-seeking economy. Elites will seek to increase the share of existing wealth without creating new wealth and at the expense of everyone else. They will secure their ability to do so through political means by, deregulation, lowering taxes and in the end weakening democracies.[8] Economic historian Bas van Bavel has shown that historically entrepreneurial egalitarian societies evolve into rent-seeking oligarchies.[9] And more worryingly, the correcting mechanism seems to be major catastrophes, usually war. This is what Martin Scheidel calls the "Great Leveler."[10] This supports Piketty's argument that the great levelers of the 20th century were the two World Wars.

6 Keay, D. (1987, October 31). Aids, Education and the Year 2000! *Woman's Own*.

7 Piketty, T. (2014). *Capital in the 21st Century*. Cambridge, MA: Harvard University Press.

8 Rodrik, D. (2017). Populism and the Economics of Globalization. *Draft*: 1–43 and Streeck, W. (2016). *How Will Capitalism End?* Verso Books.

9 Van Bavel, B. (2016). *The Invisible Hand: How Market Economies Have Emerged and Declined since AD 500*. Oxford: Oxford University Press.

10 Scheidel, W. (2017). *The Great Leveler: Violence and the History of Inequality from the Stone Age to the Twenty-First Century*. Princeton, NJ: Princeton University Press.

The West produced a social-democratic welfare system that created unprecedented opportunities and equality for a lot of people in the West (but kept an unequal and unsustainable global system intact). A capitalist system with strong state interventions and public goods. But we are increasingly finding that we are facing, what economist Danni Rodrik calls, a fundamental "trilemma": that we cannot simultaneously pursue democracy, national self-determination and economic globalization.[11] Even in the pages of pro free-market publications like the *Financial Times* and the *Economist,* these problems are now acknowledged and discussed widely.[12]

These forces are closely linked to what Samuel Huntington has defined as political decay, the decline of our institutions. Institutions, according to Huntington, are "stable, valued, recurring patterns of behaviour whose most important function is to facilitate human collective action."[13] Of course, political decay is not necessarily a bad thing, institutions need to change and adapt to accommodate changing needs of societies:

> Socioeconomic modernization led to the mobilization of new social groups over time, whose participation could not be accommodated by existing political institutions. The source of political decay was thus the inability of institutions to adapt to changing circumstances – specifically, the rise of new social groups and their political demands.

In *The Fourth Industrial Revolution,* Klaus Schwab channels Huntington with his call for new institutions, networks and new forms of collaboration.[14]

What we are witnessing now is not the rise of new social groups and institutions to support them for the benefit of us all, but the capture of states by rent-seeking elites. This has led to the steady dismantling of public institutions, including well-funded quality public education for all. In the Global South, the International Monetary Fund and World Bank have relentlessly pushed for market reforms, deregulation which in turn has weakened public institutions.[15] Those that have not gone

11 Rodrik, D. (2012). *The Globalization Paradox.* Oxford: Oxford University Press.
12 Wolf, M. (2016). Capitalism and Democracy: The Strain Is Showing. *Financial Times.*
13 Fukuyama, F. (2014). *Political Order and Political Decay.* New York: Farrar, Straus and Giroux.
14 Schwab, K. (2016). *The Fourth Industrial Revolution.* UK: Penguin.
15 Naomi, K. (2008). *The Shock Doctrine: The Rise of Disaster Capitalism.* New York: Picador.

along with these "remedies," China being a prime example, have actually prospered.[16]

Two major global trends in the global economy – globalization and automation – have sped up this process and severely impacted societies worldwide. Globalization has led to more efficient international division of labour and allocation of capital. Automation has led to increased productivity, all spurring global growth and actually lifting many people out of poverty on an unprecedented scale, but at the same time both have contributed to rising inequality in the developed world and now increasingly in the developing world as well. Globalization in its current state is not viable anymore and is leading to insecurity, political instability nationally, a fracturing of international order and a resurgence of authoritarianism in the Global South and North.[17]

We can't discuss the future of education and our profession without acknowledging this wider context. We need to recognize that if we really want to create a sustainable society, there are many domains which are public goods – literally *for the common good* – which have value on their own terms and that we need to preserve them. With public education being arguably the most important one. In contrast to Margaret Thatcher, I do believe that there is such a thing as society. I see it around me, especially in school, every day.

Flipping the System

Of course, these policies have heavily influenced education as well. Neoliberalism is a notoriously difficult beast to define and has become a catch-all phrase for everything that is wrong with society. But at the same time, it has been thoroughly researched and commented upon.[18] Stephen Ball in *Flip the System* defines neoliberalism as

neoliberalism with a big 'N', that focuses on the economization of social life and the creation of new opportunities for profit, and neoliberalism with a small 'n', through the reconfiguring of

16 Rodrik, D. (2012). *The Globalization Paradox*. Oxford: Oxford University Press.
17 Mishra, P. (2017). *Age of Anger: A History of the Present*. New York: Farrar, Straus and Giroux.
18 See for example Barker, T. (2014). Spontaneous Order: Looking Back at Neoliberalism. *Dissent*, 61(1): 91–4. Retrieved from www.dissentmagazine.org/article/spontaneous-order-looking-back-at-neoliberalism; and Amable, B. (2010). Morals and Politics in the Ideology of Neo-Liberalism. *Socio-Economic Review*, 9(1): 3–30.

relationships between the governing and the governed, power and knowledge and sovereignty and territoriality. Neoliberalism is about both money and minds.[19]

It is not a global conspiracy as some have mockingly dismissed it, but a set of economic policy beliefs, ideas and practices which have spread over the last 40 years reshaping societies and institutions around the world. Economist Danni Rodrik has called it *"a perversion of mainstream economic thinking, always more markets, always less government."*[20] Sadly I have experienced this myself in the classroom with increased competition between schools and small narrow outcomes increasingly forced me to teach a narrow history curriculum closely linked to exam results, forcing me to do what was good for the school instead of what was good for the child. This is what Dennis Shirley means when he talks about the ideological and imperial imperative.

And these ideas have spread around the world. Pasi Sahlberg has called this the Global Education Reform Movement (GERM).[21] In the Dutch case, the economization of social life and public goods meant bringing market practices and a business-efficiency mindset into public education. Schools were encouraged to compete with each other and emulate business practices, also called new public management (NPM).[22] Efficiency and effectiveness were the new buzzwords. But the questions – efficient for whom and effective for what? – weren't asked. These practices lead to a damaging cycle that eroded public education and increasingly deprofessionalized teachers. On a school level, we experienced increasing top-down managerialism, teaching to the test and a narrowing of the curriculum. School autonomy, historically one of the Dutch strong points, meant increasingly autonomy for unelected non-profit private school boards, leaving teachers and parents stranded in a democratically unaccountable system. Test scores, metrics and the reputations of educational institutions became more important than students. Students who were somehow a risk to these

---

19 Kneyber, R. (2015). On Neoliberalism and How It Travels Interview with Stephen Ball. In *Flip the System: Changing Education from the Ground Up*. Abingdon, UK: Routledge.
20 Rodrik, D. (2017). Rescuing Economics from Neoliberalism. *Boston Review*. Retrieved from http://bostonreview.net/class-inequality/dani-rodrik-rescuing-economics-neoliberalism
21 Hargreaves, A. & Shirley, D. (2012). *The Global Fourth Way: The Quest for Excellence*. Boston: Corwin Press.
22 Visser, A. (2013). Marktfilosofie en onderwijsutopie. In J. Evers & R. Kneyber (Eds.), *Het Alternatief: weg met de afrekencultuur in het onderwijs* (pp. 19–29). Amsterdam: Boom.

metrics were pushed out of the school, and schools were finding inventive ways to increase selection. The results have been worrying to say the least; one of the best and equitable education systems in the world has become more inequitable at alarming speed.[23]

There is no evidence, if you look at student outcomes on the PISA (The Programme for International Student Assessment) tests, that private schools perform better than public schools, and actually they perform worse if you factor in students' socioeconomic background. "On average across OECD countries, students in public schools score higher than students in private schools," writes the OECD.[24] In recent studies schools-voucher programs in the United States have also underperformed.[25] Yong Zhao has argued that we need to look at side effects in educational research not just at student outcomes.[26] And in the case of privatization, this is well warranted. If you look at the cost to the wider system the picture becomes a lot bleaker: school segregation, widening inequality, grade inflation, devaluation of teachers' professional judgement and the casualization of teachers through short-term contracts with low wages.[27] These effects have been well documented in the United States, Chile and Sweden for example.[28] It is not just about test scores, maybe most importantly it erodes yet another public institution, just when we need it the most.

But as Dennis Shirley also argued in the new imperatives for educational change, there is another way. In *Flip the System,* we propose to build our education systems on the basis of democratic principles and collective autonomy. We put the traditional hierarchical pyramid on its head and teachers in the lead. A move from a system of accountability to responsibility. A system where teachers are trusted instead of controlled. A system where teachers can lead on every level of the educational system. This also means treating teachers as valued professionals

23 Onderwijsinspectie. (2017). *Onderwijsverslag: De Staat van het Onderwijs.* Utrecht.
24 OECD. (2016). *PISA 2015 Results (Volume II) Policies and Practices for Successful Schools.* Paris: OECD Publishing. p. 126.
25 Montgommery,P. (2017,August3).OnVoucherstheEvidenceIsinandItIs NotGood.*Newsday.* Retrieved from www.newsday.com/opinion/commentary/on-vouchers-the-evidence-is-in-and-it-s-not-good-1.13920066
26 Zhao,Y. (2017). What Works May Hurt: Side Effects in Education. *Journal of Educational Change*: 1–21.
27 Shirley, D. (2016). *The New Imperatives of Educational Change.* New York: Routledge.
28 Adamson, F. (2016). In B. Astrand & L. Darling-Hammond, L., *Global Education Reform: How Privatization and Public Investment Influence Education Outcomes.*

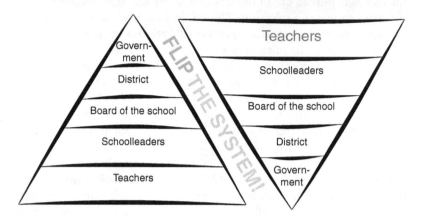

Figure 8.1   Adapted from Evers, J. & Kneyber, R, (2015). *Flip the system: changing education from the ground up.* London, Routledge.

and not as cheap, standardized and disposable labour. It means that teachers need a manageable workload and a decent standard of living. This should be a given in any educational system.

But to flip the system doesn't just mean holding up a mirror to policy makers, it also means holding up a mirror to ourselves. Teachers have to regain their *professional honour* and reconnect with the broad purpose of education.[29] Teachers have allowed these toxic systems to flourish as well. They have been going along with a lot of day-to-day practices which are detrimental for students. Teachers, and other professionals, have too often turned into "voluntary slaves," looking at someone else – politicians – to save them. To be a professional literally means to profess publicly, to go beyond your own work and take responsibility for all students and the whole. The consequence of this is that on a wider-level teachers have to organize themselves as a profession in unions and professional associations; teacher unions increasingly perform both. Instead of vilifying those institutions – a prominent feature in American educational reform – we need to strengthen and support them.

Flipping the system should more resemble a process of emancipation than a 'system intervention', a process where the 'voice' of teachers is given a meaningful place. However, the process

29 Klein, N. (2008). *The Shock Doctrine: The Rise of Disaster Capitalism.* Penguin.

cannot originate from a starting point of inequality, with teachers attempting to overcome this inequality. Teachers should instead act on an assumption of being equal, refusing and interrupting the working of powers in the educational system and laying claim to positions and discretional space that they have not previously been entitled to. To initiate this process, it is not simply a question of the government telling teachers to emancipate. It is rather a question of teachers initiating this process themselves.[30]

If there hadn't been a pedagogical void in the last 20 years, market ideas that are alien to education wouldn't have entered our schools. If you stand for nothing, you will fall for everything. So, teachers must rediscover the language of teaching and reconnect with the purpose of education. We need to ensure that our children are employable, yes, but we need to educate them as democratic citizens as well. And they need to learn and reflect on who they are, the world around them and their place in it. They need to learn to take responsibility for it. In Chapter 4, Armand showcased the Teach ME model which should be a platform to launch further discussion. We need to embrace what Gert Biesta calls "the beautiful risk of education." These are profoundly normative questions which call for ethical judgements, not standardization. It follows that we need teachers with authority (in the sense of respect) and expertise to make those professional judgements. And professional teachers means well-educated and qualified teachers.

But to teach with the mind, soul and heart, we should go beyond "teacher training" – I don't like the word – and encourage teacher education, based on a broad and holistic curriculum. Teachers should be well versed in the subjects that they teach, educated in cognitive sciences, pedagogy, philosophy history and sociology. Teachers need to read both ED Hirsch and Paolo Freire, Dylan William and Gert Biesta. And hopefully more educational academics and thinkers from the Global South – a blind spot in my own education.

Education, Teachers and Technology in the Fourth Industrial Revolution

You might have seen one of those TED Talks or read one of those clickbait blogposts with the "are we educating our kids for jobs that

30 Evers, J. & Kneyber, R. (2015). *Flip the System: Changing Education from the Ground Up.* Abingdon, UK: Routledge, p. 19.

don't exist yet?" shtick (as if the future was knowable in the past). It is one of those memes that Silicon Valley keeps pushing out to illustrate the need to "disrupt" our education system. This is a false narrative, based on a faulty premise. We never know the future completely of course, and a lot of jobs will probably look like what they do now.[31] And we actually do have a pretty clear idea what our societies might look like in the near future. Communities should not be disrupted; they should evolve. With those in the communities having a real say in the direction and its purpose. So, why do we these discourses all around us?

One reason is techno-utopism, or what Evgeny Morozov calls solutionism.[32] A real belief that technology will solve every problem without taking into account the political, social and economical intricacies involved. Another reason: qualified teachers; qualified teachers are expensive. When we talk about the teacher crisis, we need 69 million qualified teachers. This means huge investments in public education. Or not. We could also solve this by making education more efficient (sounds familiar?) or even replace teachers. Privatization in education has evolved in recent years into what might be called GERM 2.0, or the Uberfication of education. Already in the early 2000s the Swedish *Kunskapskolan* for profit company pioneered with schools using personalization and educational technology to lower the costs of teaching. "We do not mind being the McDonalds of Education," said one of its CEOs.[33] Now these ideas are spreading to the Global South where educational technology is married to low-fee for profit schools, venture capital and multinationals like Pearson. The premise is that an untrained instructor who follows a second-by-second script can provide a quality education. But Armand clearly explains in Chapter 6 that this is not what personalization in education should be about.

Old progressive ideas dating from John Dewey's time have been repurposed into an automated, "personalized" Silicon Valley vision of education. But as Audrey Watters points out in *The Automated Teacher*,

---

31 Many jobs won't be disrupted. Autor, D. H. (2015). Why Are There Still So Many Jobs? The History and Future of Workplace Automation. *Journal of Economic Perspectives*, 29(3): 3–30; and Arntz, M., Gregory, T. & Zierahn, U. (2016) *The Risk of Automation for Jobs in OECD Countries*.

32 Morozov, E. (2014). *To Save Everything, Click Here: Technology, Solutionism, and the Urge to Fix Problems That Don't Exist*. London: Penguin.

33 A Swedish Firm Has Worked Out How to Make Money Running Free Schools. (2008, June 12). *The Economist*.

these are not new ideas. In 1924, Sidney Pressey was already trying to sell a machine replacing teachers and *enhancing* learning.[34] This techno-fantasy has propped up repeatedly in the last century. And now in what some people call the great unbundling of education it is back in a new form. The future of the teaching profession, indeed of many professions, has been called in doubt due to automation and new information and communication technologies which will unbundle professions and replace them, according to writers like Daniel and Richard Susskind in *The Future of the Professions*.[35] But will they really?

The innovations that the Susskinds and others describe are augmentations at best. MOOCs feature heavily in this disrupted future for example. But recently Udacity-a MOOC pioneer and provider, Vice President Clarissa Shen, said, "MOOCs are dead."[36] And the much-touted Alt-Schools have recently shifted from opening their own schools to selling their platform to other schools. But, as parents said on Alt-School,

> their children benefitted more from the extensive attention of talented teachers and small class sizes. There are multiple instructors per class, and the school places a premium on interdisciplinary projects, like building a model house that can withstand different weather – a task that incorporates current events, science, engineering and budgeting.[37]

They describe what we need to do in a few sentences. No disruption and unbundling to be found.

In my view, McDonalds and Uber represent exactly what we mustn't do to reach the Sustainable Development Goals in 2030. As opposed to what many would have us believe these are all profound political questions, decided and acted upon by democratic societies, not some force of nature. I'm not a Luddite. I'm using technology ubiquitously

34 Watters, A. (2015, February 4). The Automatic Teacher. *Hack Education*. Retrieved from http://hackeducation.com/2015/02/04/the-automatic-teacher

35 Susskind, R. & Susskind, D. (2015). *The Future of the Professions*. Oxford: Oxford University Press.

36 Warner, J. (2017, October 11). MOOCS Are Dead. *Inside Higher Ed*. Retrieved from www.insidehighered.com/blogs/just-visiting/moocs-are-dead-whats-next-uh-oh

37 Satariano, A. (2017, November 1). Silicon Valley Tried to Reinvent Schools. Now It's Rebooting. *Bloomberg*. Retrieved from www.bloomberg.com/news/articles/2017-11-01/silicon-valley-tried-to-reinvent-schools-now-it-s-rebooting

myself, I wouldn't be here writing this book without access to social media for example. I also use technology a lot more in the classroom than the average teacher. And of course, there are many wonderful examples in this book. The role that EdTech and the companies selling it are playing in education and the narrative it has supported are worrying. I also enjoy living in a capitalistic society. But at the same time in a democratic and equal one as well. And as a citizen and as a teacher, I like to have a say in what is going on in our classrooms. That's what we have to keep in mind as we think about education and build new institutions.

Global Networks and the Networked Teacher

Crucial to achieving a flipped system is enhancing teacher agency. And we know that networking plays a crucial role in fostering this. Teacher networks within the school and professional and networks outside of the schools. I am part of many formal and informal networks. All over the world, Teach Meets, Meetups, Edcamps are springing up. There are many examples of teachers organizing their own professional development. I've probably learned the most by being part of a global professional conversation on Twitter. The best professional development of teachers is closely linked to their practice, the same goes for school and systems change. As David Frost and John Bangs write in *Flip the System*: "We have to create networking arrangements that enable teachers not only to build professional knowledge together but also to inspire each other to act strategically to bring about change."[38]

But there is also an activist component to this. The last couple of years teachers – myself included – in the Netherlands have increasingly influenced educational policy. Twitter, especially, is a powerful medium to reach politicians, journalists, researchers, but also each other.[39] Recently, in the space of a couple of months a few primary school teachers in the Netherlands have managed to organize a national movement through a Facebook group to improve the working conditions of primary teachers. They managed to organize a national strike with a 95 per cent turnout,

38 Bangs, J. & David, F. (2015). Non-Positional Leadership. In J. Evers & R. Kneyber, *Flip the System: Changing Education from the Ground Up*. Abingdon, UK: Routledge.
39 Cornelisse, F. (2015). Geflipt leiderschap is zo gek nog niet: informeel leiding nemen in collegiale netwerken binnen en buiten de school. In R. Kneyber & J. Evers, *Het Alternatief 2: de ladder naar autonomie*. Utrecht: Phronese.

not only by remaining a grassroots informal group, but by building a coalition with unions and other stakeholders. In this they show us the way forward.

We have to look at how we organize ourselves. Already in the 1966, International Labour Organization (ILO)/United Nations Educational, Scientific and Cultural Organization (UNESCO) "Recommendation concerning the Status of Teachers," it was recommended that teacher unions play a crucial role in educational policy.[40] And recently this has been echoed by the OECD and UNESCO. It was something I realized a bit later in my career. Teachers will not flip the system unless, and until, they organize collectively. But if we want to effect change we need democratic and well-organized organizations who can advocate and take action on our behalf. And most crucially provide a conduit to take action ourselves.

At the global level, teachers are already democratically organized through Education International (EI), a federation of teacher unions and professional associations. Representing 32 million teachers, it is working on capacity building for its members in the Global South and North. EI is leading the way in union renewal. In their study "Organising Teaching: developing the power of the profession," Nina Bascia and Howard Stevenson show us what that could look like.[41] We need, they argue, to focus on professional and industrial issues, build new alliances, build new networks and organize more horizontally and democratically and leverage new technologies. We now have the means to truly build an independent global teacher movement and other stakeholders should foster this.

I think it is possible to reach the goal of recruiting 69 million teachers to the profession. Not by following the advice to use technology to teach poor kids in the Global South and create a multi-tiered system where only affluent kids have access to small classes and qualified teachers.[42] This is unsustainable, because as Jong Dewey said: "What the best and wisest parent wants for his own child that must the

40 ILO. (2008). *The ILO/UNESCO Recommendation Concerning the Status of Teachers (1966) and The UNESCO Recommendation Concerning the Status of Higher-Education Teaching Personnel (1997)s*. Paris: ILO/UNESCO.
41 Bascia, N. & Stevenson, H. (2017). *Organizing Teaching: Developing the Power of the Profession*. Brussels: Education International.
42 Steed, M. (2019, December 19). Robots, Virtual Reality and the Future of Education. *The National*. Retrieved from www.thenational.ae/opinion/robots-virtual-reality-and-the-future-of-education-1.186853

community want for all of its children. Any other ideal for our schools is narrow and unlovely; acted upon, it destroys our democracy."[43] There are enough funds to pay for a good education for all children worldwide. As Stephen Klees points out:

> Globally, revenue losses due to multinational corporate tax manipulation is estimated at or above US$600 billion annually. Revenue losses on income taxes due to undeclared offshore wealth, meanwhile, are estimated to approach US$200 billion. Progress in these two areas – which will depend in large part on global countermeasures – can make a vital contribution to closing the domestic revenue gap.[44]

We do need to advocate for this though. And to do that we need to organize and to apply pressure where necessary.

We need to build our classrooms, schools and educational systems based on the principles of collaboration and trust. To do that, we need to build new institutions or reform those that aren't fit for purpose anymore. We should marry the informal to the formal, leveraging the good things social media has to offer, but not be chained by it. And this also means that we should leverage existing networks and rebuild them on principles of democracy. To achieve that we need to see teachers in a new light. We need to work on a new paradigm for teachers: the networked activist teacher. Teachers who teach, network and advocate for their students worldwide.

The Promise of the Present Moment

Earlier this year, when we reconvened after the first lesson and after some deliberation we decided, as a class, to use Timothy Snyder's "On Tyranny: twenty lessons from the twentieth century" as a guide.[45] This was a book Snyder wrote as a response to the 2016 US elections. We are going to use his 20 lessons – defend institutions, remember professional ethics, be as courageous as you can – from the 20th century as a

43 Dewey, J. (2008; originally published in 1899). *The School and Society*. New York.
44 Ron Balsera, M., Klees, S. J. & Archer, D. (2017). Financing Education: Why Should Tax Justice Be Part of the Solution? *Compare: A Journal of Comparative and International Education*: 1–16.
45 Snyder, T. (2017). *On Tyranny*. Tim Duggan Books.

framework to explore the parallels of our present day with the darkest days of the 20th century, the rise of totalitarianism, fascism and communism. We are going to reflect, connect, write, analyses, blog and podcast on the impact of the present on their daily lives and their role in the world. We will learn together, and my hope is that we will see this as "not the end, but a beginning."[46] Hopefully they will learn to take responsibility for this world.

Some viewpoints expressed here might be controversial to some, but if we are really serious about tackling the challenges of the Fourth Industrial Revolution, then we need to have these forthright discussions. With *Flip the System,* we held up a mirror to everyone: politicians, civil servants and administrators. But also, ourselves: Are we as teachers doing what is just and good for our students and society? And often the answer is no we are not. That same question should be reflected upon by other actors in education: business leaders, start-up founders, venture capitalists, think tanks, social entrepreneurs, philanthropic foundations. Are we doing what is just and good for for all the children in the world and society as a whole? And again, the answer often is no.

If we remain on the current trajectory, we will only sustain and deepen inequalities and risk global conflict. It is only by tackling these issues that we are going build new public institutions. So, hopefully in this chapter, I am taking responsibility for the present moment and the promise that it brings. In that spirit I'd like to finish with the quote by Hilel the Elder that inspired *Flip the System*:

> *If I am not for myself, who will be for me? But if I am only for myself, who am I? If not now, when?*

46 Snyder, T. (2017). *On Tyrrany*. Tim Duggan Books, p. 126.

Conclusion

Armand Doucet and Jelmer Evers

To stand at the precipice staring out to the unknown is both exhilarating and terrifying. The Fourth Industrial Revolution is rising before us. One path to the future is full of hope and optimism, while another leads to a very dark place for our global society. Over the next few years, we will face many critical choices as we stand at this crossroad.

New technological advancements offer us applications to alleviate human suffering or to further widen equity gaps. Indeed, these technological promises have brought a myriad of opportunity, but also the danger of insurmountable cost – especially for the poorest among the poor. Collectively, we must choose what we value. Which of these applications will we pursue? What motivation will drive innovation in the future? What values will we pass to our next generation? The answer to these questions will take us down one of those two paths. Education will be at the heart of these decisions.

Vikas Pota, CEO of Varkey Foundation, writes, in a 2017 TES article[1] that, in Sub Saharan Africa,

> more than a fifth of primary-age children are out of school. However, the challenge is not just at the level of school coverage: in many countries, teachers are poorly trained and supported, meaning that learning outcomes are poor. The effect of this is that around 175 million young people in poor countries – equivalent to one quarter of the youth population – cannot read a sentence.

1 Potas, V. (2017). The Failure to Educate a Child Anywhere in the World Risks Instability for Us All. Retrieved November 8, 2017, from www.tes.com/news/school-news/ breaking-views/failure-educate-a-child-anywhere-world-risks-instability-us-all

Around the world teachers are having a positive impact on their students' lives. Around the world, people are vested in our education systems because they are vested in their future. Around the world, the importance of education is understood. Unfortunately, we often fail to act on what we know to be true. Our collective actions as a society have not yet been adequate to reach the fourth United Nations Sustainable Development Goal of providing quality education to all children. And still, as Vikas Pota has stated, "regrettably, education is often thought of as something to be addressed only once poverty has been eradicated, hunger ended and health care improved. Yet, none of these problems can be fully remedied without reliable, quality education provision."[2]

As we mentioned in our introduction, Klaus Schwab rightly says, we need to build new institutions, new governance, new networks and new leadership that foster trust and can create sustainable change in our societies. "In the end, it comes down to people, culture and values."[3] He identifies four different types of intelligences that he sees as crucial in overcoming the enormous challenges ahead: contextual, emotional, inspired and physical.

Contextual (the mind) Intelligence is about how we understand and apply our knowledge, about how we must break through existing silos. Solutions to "wicked problems" like climate change "requires collaboration across boundaries with leaders from business, government, civil society, faith, and academia."[4]

As we enter a new age of Renaissance in education, it is key that in each educational jurisdiction, we align our vision to what is truly happening in the classroom, what the teachers see on the front line. Gone are the days of top-down leadership to make education work. It needs to be a collaboration with strong voices at every level, helping education move forward. That includes teachers in the classroom. Ed Catmull, the renowned creative leader behind Pixar dominance and Disney's rebirth, once said: "If there is more truth in the hallways than in meetings, you have a problem."[5]

2 Potas, V. (2017). The Failure to Educate a Child Anywhere in the World Risks Instability for Us All. Retrieved November 8, 2017, from www.tes.com/news/school-news/breaking-views/failure-educate-a-child-anywhere-world-risks-instability-us-all
3 Schwab, K. (2017). *The Fourth Industrial Revolution*. UK: Penguin.
4 Schwab, K. (2017). *The Fourth Industrial Revolution*. UK: Penguin.
5 Catmull, E. & Wallace, A. (2014). *Creativity Inc. Overcoming Unforeseen Forces That Stand in the Way of True Inspiration*. Canada: Random House.

For far too long, this has been the truth in education. Teachers are aware of the issues we are in the front line. Instead of being heard in our own educational jurisdictions, we seem to be lost in the continual search of the next best thing, which puts the system always in flux. Don't misunderstand our statement, we do believe there is a need for change, but teachers must play an integral part in it. The biggest issue within only the educational context is that our vision and mission is not aligned with the realities of the pressures of standardized testing, the accountability linked to it and that money is allocated in certain systems to only high-performing schools. That pressure is real for teachers around the world. This competitive model works for capitalism, but is horrendous for education. We answer to too many bosses, with too many differing agendas. The reality is that the only boss that should matter is the development of each child.

We are not against standardization, testing or accountability. Actually, we believe that they are important. However, we cannot use data to push agendas. Decisions need to be founded on the interpretive imperative, which states that while we should not discard data and evidence, it must be engaged with evidence on all levels – including qualitative data in the classroom. You can't only take test scores as a basis to make decisions without looking at the whole picture. Quantitative data is key, we don't disagree, but we teach humans, which means that qualitative data is just as important. The two together can give us a truer picture. We say truer picture because humans will adapt to the data collection process which skews the data itself, so the type of data is important depending on what we are looking for as teachers.

Professional teachers make calls every day on all the data they gather, and this is where technology integration can be very useful: It can show us what works and what doesn't; it can connect us to the world to create true networks with teachers and other sectors to thrive.

Emotional (the heart) intelligence is about "how we process and integrate our thoughts and feelings and relate to ourselves and to one another. Skills like self-awareness, self-regulation, motivation, empathy and social skills are essential."[6]

The Teach ME model gives teachers a template to start the discussion on how to better reach each child in the classroom. But education is not done alone. Every element that impacts a child plays a part, and the stakeholders who own each element must play their role to

6 Schwab, K. (2017). *The Fourth Industrial Revolution*. UK: Penguin.

give the child a complete education. Many are out of the control of most teachers, including food, mental health, finances, social-emotional support at home, no early childhood education, community issues, disabilities, conflict, gender identity, transgenerational abuse, poverty, prejudice, culture, faith and technology.

Governments need to take a holistic approach to raising and educating our children at the Fourth Industrial Revolution. Take a look at Finland, Singapore, Japan, Canada and New Zealand, some of the countries that rank high in some or all areas in PISA. They have strong health care systems, social systems and structured institutions that help education with all the "other" aspects that need to be taken care of for teachers to do their job. Although it is also true that not all high-performing countries have strong institutions to support education this way, and that not all countries with strong institutions rank high or very high in PISA, we believe that education, health and social support systems need to be more intertwined and orchestrated to achieve more holistic measures of education outcomes.

We need to re-think what is important to us and how we are all going to live together. Stephen Hawking gives us 50 more years on this planet if we keep going the way we are at the moment. The United Nations have created the 17 Sustainable Development goals: collaborative, multinational objectives that need to be addressed collectively and individually. We don't get where we need to go unless our societies are structured to help every step along the way.

Every educational context is different around the world, and they should be. We want all cultures to flourish in the Fourth Industrial Revolution. We don't want to see mass assimilation, which is a risk with globalization, as every culture has its own beauty. Despite the beauty of diversity, there are some universal rights that should be respected throughout the world. Education is one of those foundational rights. The Teach ME model is universal no matter what your realities are in your jurisdiction. What will be different, is how you get there based on the strengths and weaknesses of your region. The Finland model will not work around the world in a "copy/paste" format. You can't, nor would you want to, import the whole culture upon which the model is designed. However, many aspects of the Finnish model – and others – can be taken and made your own so that it works for your society.

"The sign of an educated mind is to be able to entertain an idea while not necessarily believing it," said Aristotle. If we are going to solve the Sustainable Development Goals challenge, if we are going to survive longer than 50 years, then we need to entertain ideas in each of our educational jurisdictions. We need to make sound decisions as teachers on the best way forward for our collective children, while understanding that all these problems will need global collaboration. None are isolated, no one is an island and no one stands a chance for resolution without collective efforts.

Inspired (the soul) intelligence is about "how we use a sense of individual and shared purpose, trust, and other virtues to effect change and act towards the common good."

As we found during our discussions, we have too many binary conversations in education on a range of topics when in reality we could have a place for the many sides of an argument. It doesn't always have to be black or white.

There are many ways for great education to happen. It's all about excellence. Whatever our choices, we need to fully and passionately commit to getting the very best outcomes that are possible, and then some more.

To solve the education woes of the next century, we will also need to make sacrifices. For example, it will take more than a traditional answer to address the expected 69 million teacher shortage.

As a consensus, it seems that we have recognized that children should be at the center of every education process, with teachers standing beside them as mentors and guides. Technology integration must happen, and in many places, it is already happening, for us to enhance society. It has to happen without undermining the importance of teachers. We need pedagogically empowered educators, raised, as opposed to diminished, by the opportunities presented by technology.

For this to happen, we need to re-think and re-design how we educate our teachers and re-train our existing staff. They need training on teaching to the whole child, including character, competencies, literacies and the 4Ls. We understand that teachers should not be the owners of every aspect of raising the child, but it is true that we play a very large part in each aspect.

We need to align vision from leadership with what is happening in the classroom. These new standards for teachers should be universal. It is a privilege, a calling and a profession to be a teacher. It must be treated as such, giving teachers the same respect given to professionals in other realms of all society. This is key, otherwise, the equity gaps could grow around the world and leave us in a new Dark Age.

Teaching is not an exact science, because, quite simply, humans are involved. So, the challenges facing education during the Fourth Industrial Revolution must have a holistic view from the leadership and collaboration at government level, to the design of our educational system to what we do in the classroom.

Physical (the body) intelligence is about how "we cultivate and maintain our personal health and wellbeing and that of those around us to be in a position to apply the energy required for both individual and systems transformation."

Education is a reflection of society and therefore, it is as varied and diverse as are the many societies that conform our global cultures. We can find schools, systems and even whole countries thriving or struggling anywhere in the world. Education has the potential to be the great equalizer if the child is holistically taken care of. Contextualizing education to all children individually will personalize their path throughout their formative years and give them the ability to play a large role in their communities going forward.

Education is often used as the scapegoat and the catchphrase to any problem that we face. Reality is much more complex. Yes, education should be at the core of any proposed solutions, but none will fully work unless all actors are on call. Take health, for example. We have rising cases of diabetes around the world, billions are pumped in search of miracle treatments and into hospital care. We are putting a band aid on the situation. We know how to reduce the likelihood of getting diabetes. Exercise and proper nutrition are crucial. Yet there is a growing trend of cutting or shortening physical education in many schools around the world. We might be telling our children to eat healthy, yet some families can't afford proper nutrition. We can't just dump all this on education. Teachers understand the context of their communities and can take an active role to address many of these problems. Stephen Ritz chose to teach his students how to grow their own food at school, but we can't do it alone.

Along the pages of this book, we have raised our collective voices, coming from every corner of the world, on behalf of our children. We have recognized the arrival of the Fourth Industrial Revolution, and described its implications for education today and beyond. We have presented a collection of snapshots in an attempt to better understand the vast experiences coming to life in our schools. We have confronted the reality of inequity and have explored our role as educators to address the problem. We have discussed the importance of teachers and how we need to empower them, technologically and pedagogically. We have pointed our finger to the need of flipping the system, allowing educators to lead the way for better public policies. We have marveled at the endless possibilities of integrating technology in our classrooms, and shared concrete and practical examples from outstanding teachers. We have demanded from society to jump in and fulfill its calling, embracing our schools and supporting our children while they strive to reach their potential.

Our voices express ideas that might not be new. Many might have heard them in the past, but very few have listened. These voices are not aimed at proposing one-size-fits-all kind of solutions. In fact, we humbly recognize that most answers to today's challenges are still to be found. It is our hope that our words can spark the discussions that are needed to create change.

Rather than passively wait for history to take its course, or to succumb before the inevitable shifts that come ahead, we want to inspire educators and the society in full to make active decisions and take whatever roads we need so as to guarantee that every child in the world has the opportunity to thrive.

We started this book standing at the precipice.

It is in our power to make decisions and act upon them.

Will each of us have the courage?

Epilogue

Andreas Schleicher

The Sustainable Development Goals set by the global community provide a perspective for the wellbeing of the planet by 2030. That is also the date when today's young primary school pupils will be finishing their school. As Michael and Elisa lay out in the opening chapters of this book, the road to 2030 will see more evidence of the sea-change caused by digitalization, which is connecting people, cities, countries and continents to bring together a majority of the world's population in ways that vastly increases our individual and collective potential. But as the authors of this book also point out, the same technological and economic forces have made the world also more volatile, more complex and more uncertain. The rolling processes of automation, hollowing out jobs, particularly for routine tasks, have radically altered the nature of work and life. For those with the advantage of the right human capacities, this is liberating and exciting. But for those who are insufficiently prepared, it can mean the scourge of vulnerable and insecure work, and life without prospects.

In the social and economic sphere, the questions turn on equity and inclusion. We are born with what political scientist Robert Putnam calls *bonding social capital*, a sense of belonging to our family or other people with shared experiences, cultural norms, common purposes or pursuits. But it requires deliberate and continuous effort to create the kind of *bridging social capital* through which we can share experiences, ideas and innovation and build a shared understanding among groups with diverse experiences and interests, thus increasing our radius of trust to strangers and institutions. Societies that nurture bridging social capital and pluralism have always been more creative, as they can draw on and bring to bear the best talent from anywhere, build on multiple perspectives and nurture creativity and innovation. But that, too, is being put to test these days.

Sustainability has become another dimension of the challenge. The goal declared by the Brundtland Commission some 30 years ago – calling for development that meets the needs of the present without compromising the ability of future generations to meet their own needs – is more relevant today than ever, in the face of environmental degradation, climate change, overconsumption and population growth. Already, many of our best minds are focused on building sustainable cities, developing green technologies, redesigning systems and rethinking individual lifestyles. For the young, the challenges encapsulated in the 2015 Sustainable Development Goals are often urgent, personal and inspiring.

While sustainability aims to put the world into balance, resilience looks for ways to cope in an imbalanced world, recognizing that the world exists in constant disequilibrium. These days, we no longer know exactly how things will unfold, often we are surprised and need to learn from the extraordinary, and sometimes we make mistakes along the way. And it will often be the mistakes and failures, when properly understood, that create the context for learning and growth. Strengthening cognitive, emotional and social resilience and adaptability is perhaps the most significant challenge for modern education, as it affects virtually every part of the education system. That starts with understanding that resilience is not a personality trait, but a process that can be learned and developed. In the 21st century, education is a key tool to help people, organizations and systems to persist, perhaps even thrive, amid unforeseeable disruptions. And at the collective level, education can provide communities and institutions with the flexibility, intelligence and responsiveness they need to persist in social and economic change.

So education is a key differentiator for how the next decades will play out for individuals, nations and the planet. Prior to the first industrial revolution, neither education nor technology mattered much for the vast majority of people. But when technology raced ahead of education during that period, vast numbers of people were left behind, causing unimaginable social pain. It took a century for public policy to respond with the gradual push to provide every child with access to schooling. But eventually, education got ahead of technology again. As the authors of this book analyze, it is not clear to what extent that analogy holds for our times of the fourth industrial revolution, where technology is racing ahead ever faster, but the least we should do is imagine the type of education that will help people take advantage of our times. It is likely that future jobs will *pair* computer intelligence with the social and emotional skills, attitudes and values of human beings. It will then be precisely our capacity for innovation, our awareness and our sense of responsibility that will equip us to harness machines to shape the world for the better. That is what will enable humans to create new value, which involves processes of creating, making, bringing into being and formulating and can generate outcomes that are innovative, fresh and original, contributing something of intrinsic positive worth. It suggests entrepreneurialism in the broader sense of being ready to venture, to try, without anxiety about failure. So human beings need not be passive or inert. We have agency, the ability to anticipate and to take action, and the power to frame our actions within a purpose and to devise and execute a plan to achieve that purpose.

In a structurally imbalanced world, the imperative of reconciling diverse perspectives and interests, in local settings with sometimes global implications, will require young people to become adept in handling tensions, dilemmas and trade-offs. Striking the balance, in specific circumstances, between competing demands – of equity and freedom, autonomy and community, innovation and continuity and efficiency and democratic process – will rarely lead to an either/or choice or even a single solution. Individuals will need to think in a more integrated way that avoids premature conclusions and attends to interconnections. In a 2030 world of interdependency and conflict, people will successfully secure the wellbeing of themselves, their families and their communities only by developing this second transformative competency: the capacity to reconcile their own goals and perceptions with the perspectives of others.

Last but not least, we have an obligation to distribute human potential far more equitably, and Michael makes that point so pertinently in Chapter 3. This is a moral and social obligation, but also a huge opportunity. A growth model based on human potential can produce a more dynamic economy and inclusive society, since talent is far more equally distributed than opportunity and financial capital. More equitable skills have also a complementary impact on reducing gaps in earnings. And they have this impact, while also expanding the size of the economy. That differs from simple tax and redistribution schemes that might change the distribution of incomes but do not add to the overall output.

There is another side to this, as the pace of change makes it simply no longer economically feasible and sustainable to address inequalities mainly through redistribution; we need to turn towards addressing the sources of economic inequalities, and these lie to a significant extent in the way in which we develop and use the talent of people. This core asset of our times remains hugely undervalued and it is time to unlock it. Not least, the cost of leaving people out will be to fuel simplistic political and economic responses that will hurt everyone.

The dilemma for educators is that routine cognitive skills, the skills that are easiest to teach and easiest to test, are exactly the skills that are also easiest to digitize, automate and outsource. As Armand illustrates in powerful ways in Chapter 4, educational success is no longer going to be about reproducing content knowledge, but about extrapolating from what we know and applying that knowledge creatively in novel situations, and about thinking across the boundaries of subject-matter disciplines. If everyone can search for information on the Internet, the rewards now come from what people do with that knowledge.

Similarly, the more rapidly that content knowledge evolves in a subject, the more important it is for students to understand the structural and conceptual foundations of a discipline rather than its content with a limited shelf life.

Innovation and problem solving also depend increasingly on being able to bring together disparate elements and to synthesize them to create something different and unexpected. This is about curiosity, open-mindedness, making connections between ideas that previously seemed unrelated. It requires being familiar with knowledge in a range of fields. If we spend our whole life in a silo of a single discipline, we will not gain the imaginative skills to connect the dots to see where the next invention might be found. Some countries have been trying. Japan introduced a course of integrated studies into its school curriculum in the late 1990s, but it had limited impact, particularly in secondary schooling where exams are focused on isolated disciplinary knowledge, which then shapes the priorities of students and teachers.

More recently, Finland has made project-based and cross-disciplinary learning central to all student learning experiences, posing real-life problems to students that require them, for example, to think like a scientist, think like a historian and think like a philosopher, all at the same time. But even Finland faces a major implementation gap with this goal. Students will only learn to think in multi-disciplinary ways when teachers themselves are open to the paradigms of multiple disciplines and can collaborate effectively across the boundaries of disciplines. But the fragmented organization of school days and teachers' work means that there is often limited room for such collaboration across subject divides.

The world is also no longer divided into specialists, who know a lot about very little, and generalists, who know little about a lot. Specialists generally have deep skills and narrow scope, giving them expertise that is recognized by peers, but not always valued outside their domain. Generalists have broad scope but shallow skills. What counts today are people who are able to apply depth of skill to new situations and experiences, gaining new competences, building new relationships and assuming new roles. They are not capable of constantly learning, unlearning and relearning in a fast-changing world when the contexts change. Helping students develop effective learning strategies and metacognitive abilities such as self-awareness, self-regulation and self-adaptation will become increasingly important and needs to be reflected more explicitly in curricula and instructional practice.

The more knowledge that technology allows us to search and access, the more important becomes the capacity to make sense out of this content. Students need to be able to question or seek to improve the accepted knowledge and practices. Literacy in the 20th century was about accessing and managing information. In the 21st century, it's no longer enough to tell students to look up an answer in a textbook and to assume that it will be accurate: students now need to be able to navigate conflicting information on the Internet and construct new knowledge from what they read.

Perhaps most significant are the social and emotional skills and character qualities that help us live and work together. These are skills involved in achieving goals, working with others and managing emotions. They play an indispensable and increasing role in all stages of life. Along with cognitive and learning abilities, it is important that students develop strong social and emotional skills to balance and ground their personalities, particularly given the uncertainties they face in their future. This includes character qualities such as perseverance, empathy, resilience, mindfulness, ethics, courage or leadership.

Social and emotional skills intersect in important ways with diversity. These days, schools need to become better at preparing students to live and work in a world in which most people will need to collaborate with people of different cultural origins, and appreciate a range of ideas, perspectives and values; a world in which people need to decide how to trust and collaborate across such differences, often bridging space and time through technology; and a world in which their lives will be affected by issues that transcend national boundaries.

That brings me to the toughest challenge in modern education: how to incorporate values into the instructional system. Values have always been central to education, but it is time that they move from implicit aspirations to explicit educational goals and practices in ways that help communities shift from situational values – which means "I do whatever a situation allows me to do" – to sustainable values that generate trust, social bonds and hope. Of course, values are a difficult territory for schools. To make one's way through it, one has to strike a balance between strengthening common values in societies, such as respect, empathy and tolerance, that cannot be compromised, and appreciating the diversity of our societies and the plurality of values that diversity engenders. Leaning too far in either direction is risky: enforcing an artificial uniformity of values is detrimental to people's capacity to acknowledge different perspectives, and overemphasizing diversity can lead to cultural relativism that questions the legitimacy of any core values. But avoiding this issue in discussions about the curriculum just means that it becomes another problem put on the shoulders of classroom teachers without any adequate support.

That is all easy to say, but how do we foster motivated, engaged learners who are prepared to conquer the unforeseen challenges of tomorrow, not to speak of those today? Nadia, Koen and Armand provide powerful answers to this in the second half of this book. And these answers are mirrored in some of the world's most advanced schools and education systems.

In traditional school systems, teachers have often been dispatched to the classroom with prescribed instructions about what to teach in their subject. A different model has emerged in top-performing school systems, with teachers being given the tools and the support to find their own more individual path. There are clear goals for what students should be able to do, but there is an expectation of more professional independence for how teachers achieve this.

The past was about received wisdom, the future is about user-generated wisdom. The past was divided – with teachers and content divided by subjects and students separated by expectations of their future prospects. The past could also be isolated – with schools designed to keep students inside, and the rest of the world out, with a lack engagement with families and a reluctance to partner with other schools. The future needs to be integrated – with an emphasis on the integration of subjects and the integration of students. It needs to be connected – so that learning is connected to real-world contexts and contemporary issues and open to the rich resources in the community. Instruction in the past was subject-based, instruction in the future needs to be more project-based, building experiences that help students think across the boundaries of disciplines and domains of knowledge. The past was hierarchical, the future is more collaborative, recognizing both teachers and students as resources and co-creators.

In the past, different students were taught in similar ways. Top-performing school systems embrace diversity with differentiated approaches to teaching. The past was curriculum centered, the future is learner centered. The goals of the past were standardization and compliance, with students educated in age cohorts, following the same standard curriculum, all assessed at the same time. The future is about personalizing educational experiences, building instruction from student passions and capacities, helping students to personalize their learning and assessment in ways that foster engagement and talents, and it's about encouraging students to be ingenious. As well as countering educational disadvantage, this can help capitalize on the strengths of the most talented students.

In the past, schools were technological islands, with technology often limited to supporting existing practices, and students outpacing schools in their adoption and consumption of technology. The schools of the future will use the potential of technologies to liberate learning from past conventions and connect learners in new and powerful ways, with new sources of knowledge, with innovative applications and with one another. The future will be about participating.

We need to deeply understand that learning is not a place but an activity. School systems need to recognize that individuals learn differently, and differently at different stages of their lives. They need to foster new approaches that allow people to learn in ways that are most conducive to their progress.

The focus of policy needs to be on the outcomes of a school system, rather than on arguments about how education is provided. This means shifting from looking inwards at the bureaucratic structure towards looking outwards to the next teacher, the next school, the next education system. Powerful learning environments are constantly creating synergies and finding new ways to enhance professional, social and cultural capital with others. They do that with families and communities, with higher education, with businesses, and especially with other schools and learning environments. This is about creating innovative partnerships.

These are challenging demands, and the result is that the expectations for teachers are high and rising each day. We expect them to have a deep and broad understanding of what they teach and whom they teach, because what teachers know and care about makes such a difference to student learning. But we expect much more than what we put into the job descriptions of teachers. We expect teachers to be passionate, compassionate and thoughtful; to make learning central and encourage students' engagement and responsibility; to respond effectively to students of different needs, backgrounds and languages, and to promote tolerance and social cohesion; to provide continual assessments of students and feedback; and to ensure that students feel valued and included and that learning is collaborative. And we expect teachers themselves to collaborate and work in teams, and with other schools and parents, to set common goals, and plan and monitor the attainment of goals.

Teachers of today's "connected" learners are also confronted with challenging issues around the digital world, from information overload to plagiarism, from protecting children from online risks such as fraud, violations of privacy or online bullying to setting an adequate and appropriate media diet. They are expected to help educate children to become critical consumers of Internet services and electronic media, to make informed choices and avoid harmful behaviors.

But there is more to this. Successful learners generally had a teacher who was a mentor and took a real interest in their life and aspirations, who helped them understand who they are, discover what their passions are and where they can capitalize on their specific strength; who taught them how to love to learn and build effective learning strategies as the foundation for lifelong learning; and who helped them find out where they can make a difference to social progress. Those aspects of teacher quality are difficult to compare and quantify, but designing a work organization and support culture that nurtures these qualities among teachers will give public policy a powerful handle on successful learning.

At the heart of this question is not technology, but ownership. That requires creating a teaching profession that owns its professional practice, and that puts teachers at the top and not the bottom of the pyramid, as the authors describe in Chapter 8. I meet many people who say we cannot give teachers and educational leaders greater autonomy because they lack the capacity and expertise to deliver. And that, of course, often holds some truth. But a response that simply perpetuates an industrial model of teaching will continue to disengage teachers, like someone who heats up pre-cooked hamburgers will never become a master chef.

In contrast, when teachers feel a sense of ownership over their classrooms, when students feel a sense of ownership over their learning that is when productive learning takes place. So, the answer is to strengthen trust, transparency, professional autonomy and the collaborative culture of the profession all at the same time.

Perhaps the most essential reason why teachers' ownership of the profession is a must-have rather than an optional extra lies in the pace of change in the school system. Even the most effective attempts to translate a government-established curriculum into classroom practice will drag out over a decade, because it takes so much time to communicate the goals and methods through the different layers of the system and to build them into traditional methods of teacher education.

Such a slow process is no longer good enough because it inevitably leads to a widening gap between what students need to learn and what teachers teach.

The only way to shorten the pipeline is to professionalize teaching, that is, to provide teachers not only with a deep understanding of the curriculum as a *product*, but equally with the *process* of curriculum and instructional design and the pedagogies to enact and enable the ideas behind the curriculum. Subject-matter knowledge will be less and less the core and more and more the context of good teaching.

Schools face a tough challenge in responding to changes in what will be valuable for young people in the future. The traditional content-based curriculum needs to be replaced by fast-moving flows of knowledge creation. Much of today's curricula are designed to equip learners for a static world that no longer exists. Those types of curricula could be delivered with an industrial approach. And they did not require advanced professional insights around instructional design on the part of teachers. That is no longer good enough. As the prescriptive approach weakens, the position of the classroom practitioners needs strengthening. While governments can establish directions and curriculum goals, teachers themselves need to take charge of the instructional system.

If I can add one more aspect, it is the need to look outward, for teachers to look to the next teacher, for schools to look to the next school and for education systems to look to the next education system. It is not surprising that a strong and consistent effort to carry out international benchmarking and to incorporate the results of that benchmarking into policy and practice is a common characteristic of the highest-performing education systems.

Finland was benchmarking itself against the performance and practices of other education systems in the run-up to its own dramatic emergence as one of the world's top performers. Japan launched its long-running status as one of the world's leading performers when its government, during the Meiji Restoration, visited the capitals of the industrializing West and decided to bring to Japan the best that the rest of the world had to offer. It has been doing so ever since.

When Deng Xiaoping took the helm in China and began its rise on the world's industrial stage, he directed China's education institutions to form partnerships with the best educational institutions in the world and to bring back to China the best of their policies and practices. In the latter half of the 20th century, Singapore did exactly what Japan had done a century earlier, but with even greater focus and discipline.

Contrast this outward-looking attitude with that of those countries which prefer to cast doubt over the Programme for International Student Assessment (PISA) when test results show that their education system has been outperformed and that consider it humiliating to make comparisons with what is happening in other countries.

This is likely to be a key differentiator between which countries make progress. The division will be between those education systems that feel threatened by alternative ways of thinking and those that are open to the world and ready to learn from the world's best experiences.

Index